THE
ROYALS

THE
ROYALS

LEONARD MOSLEY
AND
ROBERT HASWELL

LESLIE FREWIN : LONDON

© LEONARD MOSLEY AND ROBERT HASWELL 1966

FIRST PUBLISHED 1966
BY LESLIE FREWIN PUBLISHERS LIMITED
15 HAY'S MEWS, BERKELEY SQUARE, LONDON, W1

PRINTED BY ANCHOR PRESS
AND BOUND BY WILLIAM BRENDON
BOTH OF TIPTREE, ESSEX

CONTENTS : Introduction **11**

The book designed by H. J. Deverson

The cartoons by kind permission of *GILES*

Robert Haswell's photographs reproduced
by courtesy of the 'Daily Express'

THE ROYALS

(see page 168)

Introduction

February 1966 was the fourteenth anniversary of Queen Elizabeth the Second's accession to the throne, and the beginning of what may well be the most critical years of her reign.

This strong-minded, self-confident, healthy young woman has now ruled over Britain and the Commonwealth for only one year less than her father, King George the Sixth, and yet is still in the prime of her life, destined, one suspects, to live as long as her great-great-grandmother, Queen Victoria.

In a world which is changing as rapidly as this one, will her reign be as long – and, if so, as glorious? Or will the revolutionary challenges of the sixties threaten its stability along with the teetering and tottering pillars of the Establishment which modern attitudes, ideas and antagonisms have already undermined?

As any minister or ex-minister at Westminster will admit, Queen Elizabeth is well aware that the Monarchy is under closer scrutiny today than at any time since the reign of Edward the Seventh, though for different reasons. It was not the *institution* of the Monarchy which was criticised in Edwardian days (except by the very few) so much as the character and proclivities of its titular head. The contrary is the case today. It is the nature of the institution rather than its representative which stirs criticism now.

Can this be because, today, the Monarchy as an institution is only too vulnerable, whereas Elizabeth the Second is a personality whose qualities and values even her bitterest enemies find hard to assail?

For what do men say of the Monarchy, in Parliament, in the satirical TV programmes, in the public bars? Out of date. An expensive luxury. An anachronism geared to antediluvian traditions. Out of keeping with a modern, progressive state.

It is easy to bombard the royal system with cliché phrases like these. It is much harder to shoot down the Queen, as even polemicists such as Mr Malcolm Muggeridge have discovered. A few years ago, asked to make known his views on Elizabeth and her reign, Mr Muggeridge managed to write a whole article without once mentioning her name. His criticisms were directed not against the Queen on the throne but the idea of the Monarch in his mind; and in the course of his disquisitions he managed to deliver some remarks which were not only misguided against the system but unfairly directed at the Queen he did not name.

'With all the appurtenances of supreme authority,' he wrote, 'the Monarch has come to exercise none. Any rural district councillor, in practice, has more to say about public affairs.'

One doubts if this was ever true of royalty in the last hundred years, but it is woefully wide of the mark today. Never before has the influence of the Throne been more in evidence in the conduct of the nation's affairs. True, it has rarely been exercised in public,[1] but it is no secret that her personal influence has been increasing year by year, and that the five prime ministers with whom she has now had dealings since she came to the throne all (though it took time in some cases) came to respect her clear-headed, forthright views on foreign and domestic affairs; and that some of them came to fear the Hanoverian stubbornness with which she sometimes insisted in pushing her views down their throats.

Those who have watched her settle herself securely into the comfortable hollows of her throne would say that today she is less concerned with the effectiveness of her role behind the scenes (a role she is confident she fills well) than with her public image. Her preoccupation with ruling was instilled in her practically from birth, in the tradition of her grandfather and father before her, and she knows her obligations almost by rote – but believes them fervently: *that above all else, her duty is to her people as a whole; to remember that no matter what the political complexion (or even the simple pigment) of the government in power, it is her task to try to direct that their laws bear equally upon all; to do her best to persuade her ministers to be impartial and just; but, when a goverment asks of her a reasonable lead, to obey.*

1. The Queen's overt approval of her Government's Rhodesian policy is one of the exceptions.

Of necessity, however, people are going to judge the reign of Elizabeth not from what goes on during her private meetings with her ministers, the nature of which is not likely to be known in the lifetime of most of her subjects, but by the public personality which she and the people surrounding her present to the world, through their public speeches and appearances and through their public actions.

It should be remembered that Queen Elizabeth is not just the head of a State, but the head of an organisation as well, a business, the royalty business – in which her husband, her sons and daughter, her mother, sister, her cousins, aunts and in-laws all have stakes.

In a world which is bubbling with pink-scented, synthetic heroes and heroines, 'pop' stars, screen and TV idols, all avid for the headlines, their images pressured into public notice by powerful publicity machines, the Queen and the Royals she represents face a problem which is not easy to solve. How far can they concede to the demands of an age dedicated to advertising and public relations and allow themselves to be exposed – and still retain the aura of majesty and mystique which has, until now, always clung to royalty in this country? To what extent can they permit themselves to compete with the popular idols of the day, when they know that the popular idols are here today and gone tomorrow, are as good only as their next film, play or song, whereas the Royals are here for good?

Or is it necessary for them to compete at all? There are those officials at Buckingham Palace who have strong feelings about it. They echo the opinions of Queen Elizabeth's father, King George the Sixth, who objected to any publicity about himself or his family which was not strictly concerned with official business or public ceremonial. The Queen has not forgotten the occasion, a year before her father's death, when the Royal Family assembled at Balmoral Castle to celebrate the twenty-first birthday of her sister, Princess Margaret. Looked at from present-day standards, it would seem to have been an obvious occasion for some recognition of the interest of the public and the newspapers. It is not every day that the extremely pretty second daughter of the most powerful of the existing monarchies comes of age; and it was surely an occasion when her birthday celebrations could have been legitimately considered to be a matter of public interest. As a result, some British newspapers[1] sent photographers and reporters to pick up as best they could

1. The *Daily Express*, acting on its own behalf and also for a world-wide syndicate, was the most prominent.

13

from the moors what they were not given in the way of pictures and information from inside Balmoral. The result was both pathetic and unseemly.

With the late King's tacit encouragement, it became a game among the guests at Princess Margaret's birthday celebrations to dodge the Press by day and mock them by night. At an evening concert held in the castle, a member of the party sang a song which went as follows:

> 'If you go up to the hills today
>   You're in for a big surprise.
> If you go up to the hills today
>   You'd better go in disguise.
> For all the Press that ever was
>   Will gather there for certain because
> Today's the day that somebody has a birthday.
>
> Peeking time for Beaver boys,
>   A lovely time for Beaver boys,
> Clicking their cameras all today
>   As they ruin our holiday.'

Princess Elizabeth (as the Queen then was) enjoyed the joke with the others at the time. She laughed louder when the birthday girl herself eluded the most energetic of the scouting correspondents – an indefatigable woman reporter from the *Daily Express* – and later sang:

> 'The guns are chasing the grouses,
>   The grouses are chasing Lord E.
> The cats are chasing the mouses,
>   And Eve Perrick's chasing me!'

In similar circumstances today, however, it is highly unlikely that she would erect such a *cordon sanitaire* around her own son or daughter, and it seems certain that the coming of age of the Prince of Wales will be a national celebration, with every ounce of co-operation asked for from the newspapers, rather than the occasion for some poor parlour jokes.

But in what circumstances should publicity for the Queen and her entourage of Royals be encouraged, and to what extent should restrictions be placed upon the reporting and photographing of their activities? When is a member of the Royal Family to be considered off-duty, and is this a matter to be decided by Buckingham Palace or the Government? To what lengths should the Queen go to make sure that her relatives, who so often represent her at home and abroad, be subject in their behaviour, remarks and attitude to her supervision, as head of the royal operation?

This book is a study, in words and pictures, of the way in which the Queen and her immediate circle of relatives have been influenced in their attitudes and their public appearances by the changes in Britain and the Commonwealth over the past decade. It is an account of a quiet, but nevertheless often painful, revolution in regal behaviour and outlook; and of the way in which the Queen has tried to influence, not always successfully, the Royals who surround her to accept and adapt the circumstances which face a monarchy and its courtiers to the Britain, the Commonwealth and the world of the nineteen-sixties.

Let us then consider the task of the Queen, and look at the team with which she has to work.

The fruitful consortium

One of the more senior officials at Buckingham Palace who wrote his memoirs after he retired (though they have not so far been published) mentioned in one of the chapters that Prince Philip was 'as poor as a church mouse' when he first proposed to Princess Elizabeth.

'All he possessed,' the official wrote, 'was his uniform, a spare suit and a credit of £6.10.0 at the bank.'

Even in those days it was an inaccurate summing-up of Philip's assets. He had irrepressible youth and vigour, a remarkably potent and penetrating personality, a hard-driving toughness (half the result of his lonely childhood, half the fruit of his training at Gordonstoun and in the Royal Navy), and a furious determination to learn and do well whatever job he was given.

With fewer assets than those, men have become millionaires, prime ministers and presidents, and there is no reason to doubt that, even then, Prince Philip considered them more than sufficient for the Consort of a Queen. He has proved it to be so in the years since his marriage.

Prince Philip, Duke of Edinburgh, First Gentleman of the Realm, was forty-five years old in the spring of 1966; a power in Britain, a strong influence in the Commonwealth and a personality known and respected throughout the world. The fact that he is no longer just the Queen's Consort (as Prince Albert was to Queen Victoria) walking in Elizabeth's shadow, head deferentially bent, hands behind his back, is due in great measure to his extraordinary strength of purpose and dedication.

But it is also almost equally due to the influence of the Queen herself, and, in this case, more than is perhaps realised.

Looking back on the hopes and aspirations which motivated Philip's backers in his premarital years, one begins to realise that they could not possibly have envisaged how vital would be the eventual role of the bridegroom they had chosen for the future Queen. At the time when they espoused his cause, his position was altogether too obscure and his prospects too uncertain to give them any hint of the power-house of energy and ambition they were plugging into the royal grid.

Prince Philip had, indeed, been born a prince, but until the time of his marriage had never had the money nor the opportunity to live or act like one. The facts of his early life must, by now, be well known, and they were part of the reason why he had been chosen. Born 10 June 1921, at the Greek royal summer home of 'Mon Repos', on the island of Corfu, the son of Prince Andrew of Greece and his wife, Princess Alice. Flight nine months later from a rebellious Greece aboard a British destroyer, with his mother and four older sisters. The escape of his father from a Greek firing squad and his exile in Paris. The separation of his parents – and the gradual realisation that they had been sadly ill-matched and should really have never come together, for Andrew was a gay gadabout and Alice a religious devotee, and deaf. Philip's vagabond life as a boy, never quite knowing where his home was nor what his nationality. The influence of his two English uncles, the Marquis of Milford Haven and Lord Louis Mountbatten (later Earl Mountbatten of Burma), who gentled him through his adolescence, got him into the Navy, slowly turned him into an Englishman.

It was a disturbed and not very happy introduction to manhood, but he weathered it. With his marriage to Princess Elizabeth the question of his future was settled, and once he had been naturalised, once he had been baptised into the Church of England, once he had been married, one could almost hear his sponsors saying:

'All that boy will want from now on is peace and quiet. He has found a haven. Such a nice, quiet, amenable young man to be the husband of a Queen-to-be.'

Rarely have hopes been more devastatingly, and more happily, dashed.

To understand the Prince Philip of the nineteen-sixties, it is necessary to remember the circumstances which confronted him in the first years of his marriage.

From the start it was impressed upon him that, to win his spurs with the public, he would need to be more British than the British. 'To get out of an insane asylum,' one of his advisers told him, 'an inmate must prove to the doctors that he is twice as sane as the people outside. In a sense, your case is now being examined by Dr Britain.'

There followed periods which must have been supremely trying for him. The newspapers of the day, for instance, published the fact that his three surviving sisters (all of them married to German princelings) were, in bleak, post-war Germany, having to queue up with ordinary Germans at the food-rationing offices for their weekly allocations of bread, fats and meat. It was a time when many a German fräulein was having her larder filled by her Army acquaintances, and Philip must have been sorely tempted to help out his sisters, with whom his ties have always been close and affectionate; but he was aware that sniping critics had their sights on him and instinctive feelings of sympathy had to remain just that and nothing more than that. He had to remind himself that to the British people, only just emerging from the fires and hatreds of war, they were Germans and therefore enemies, undeserving of pity. He deliberately did nothing to alleviate the hard lot of his family, and he must have found it painful – though he more than made up for it later.[1]

In the light of his reputation in Britain today, it seems incredible that, in the first years of his marriage, the principal task of the Palace advisers was to 'build him up' with the public, and embellish his image. He was, for a time, completely unsure of himself and even allowed his assertive young sister-in-law, Princess Margaret, to push him around and patronise him. It was a time when the Queen could not do much to help, for her own life and activities were still circumscribed by the customs (or, rather, the taboos) imposed upon royal publicity by officials who were hangovers from her father's reign – men who blenched at the name of a royal personage in a newspaper in connection with anything but an official speech or occasion, whose idea of a royal photograph was a chocolate-box pose by Dorothy Wilding, who deprecated any hint that the Monarch (particularly a female Monarch)

1. In later years, whenever any of them came to London, they always found an envelope beside their bed filled with pocket-money from Philip; and he has done his best to introduce his sisters' children to anyone likely to prove a suitable match.

might occasionally be human and blow her nose, laugh out loud, or be caught with her hemline showing.

It was during this difficult interregnum that Philip's uncle, Earl Mountbatten of Burma, came to the rescue. Mountbatten had retained in his official capacity at the Admiralty the staff which had worked so ably on his behalf during the War and afterwards during his remarkable term of office as last Viceroy of India. It included some experts at public relations. He had also kept in close contact with another ex-member of his staff, Alan Campbell-Johnson, who had gone into civilian public relations. From their combined discussions came an idea which was to prove a break-through for Prince Philip in his campaign to win the solid approval of the British people. It was proposed that Earl Mountbatten should relinquish one of the many part-time positions which he held as President of the National Playing Fields Association and recommend Philip as his successor. The organisation, as a result of the war, and through no fault of Mountbatten, was rusty and its administration constricted with red-tape. It would be Philip's job to oil the machine, disentangle the bureaucracy and demonstrate it to the public as a cause worthy of their support.

It was a task after his own heart, and he galvanised all those connected with it. His work for the NPFA kept him at his desk for hours, dictating memoranda and appeals, chivvying his organisers, squeezing 'all the rich people I know for all the juice I can get out of them'. He once said: 'I'll go anywhere to open a playing field', and he did, sometimes at considerable cost to his sleeping time. Under his driving pressure, half a million pounds was raised for the fund. The remarkable thing is that he enjoyed the hard grind behind the scenes as well as the perks which went with the job. These were also enjoyable. The way to get money for charity is to organise concerts, variety shows, balls, film premières, and these brought him into contact with show-people. He was the first member of the Royal Family since King Edward's day to rub shoulders with the world of show-business, and he made no bones about showing that he liked it.

There were moments of leisure, of course, and these had their happy discoveries, too. Philip's financially restricted childhood had prevented him from indulging in those princely pursuits, shooting and riding. At the beginning of his marriage he was hardly a duffer but not very good either with a horse or a gun, a condition in British royal circles rather like being an illiterate at All Souls. The story goes that

20

the first time he went out with his father-in-law, King George the Sixth, he missed forty shots out of fifty and almost made that dedicated marksman have momentary doubts about his suitability as a match for his daughter.

Prince Philip was not too chastened. Since boyhood he has been meeting and relishing challenge.[1]

He practised long and hard with both shotgun and rifle, and turned himself into a crack shot. Some competition from the distaff side may well have spurred him on. He knew that Elizabeth was a first-class markswoman, far better than most women. He told his friends that he would not be satisfied with his progress until he was shooting as well as, if not better than, the Queen. He is, now.

So it was with horses, too. It was his uncle, Earl Mountbatten, who persuaded him to take up polo, and he worked at every spare moment to perfect his technique. After the Queen's accession and the move into Buckingham Palace, Philip rigged up a gymnasium with an electric horse and a padded wall, against which he slammed shots with his polo stick. At Windsor, where the grass has been all but sacrosanct since the days of Victoria, the Queen came out one morning to find her husband galloping a pony furiously up and down the lawn. She suggested sharply that he was ruining the turf, and Philip, belatedly realising the hallowed nature of English grass, reined in his pony and looked suitably abashed. But he went on with his exercises elsewhere.

Today he is a good, if not great, polo player, though some of his critics, perhaps jealous of the enormous zest and utter lack of fear which he displays in a game, are inclined to say that he is not so much a horseman as a user-up of horses. But his control of them is magnificent, and he gets far more out of his mounts than the Queen does from her own horses, though her deft admixture of skill and fond guidance is beautiful to watch.

During what might be called the running-in period of his life as Consort of the Queen, Prince Philip was content to do what the staider and more old-fashioned

---

1. When King George and Queen Mary visited Dartmouth Naval College in 1939 and subsequently departed in the Royal Yacht *Victoria and Albert*, Prince Philip, then a cadet of eighteen, rowed out to sea in the wake of the royal yacht and continued long after all the other cadets had turned back. Romantics nowadays say he did it because Princess Elizabeth, then twelve years old, was also aboard. It was much more likely that he was proving, as at Gordonstoun, that he was the best of the cadets and wanted his Uncle Bertie to know it.

Prince Philip rigged out for the Ascot races. But that other headgear is more to his liking . . .

When Prince Philip plays polo he gives no quarter and expects none. Someone once called him a'user-up of horses' because he drives his ponies so hard. But he is a brilliant and hard rider and makes no secret of his determination to win; and he gives short shrift to anyone who gets in his way as he gallops towards the ball. He has taken some painful tumbles but doesn't seem to mind the cuts or bruises. These photographs taken at Windsor Great Park and Cowdray Park show that he can be just as relaxed out of the saddle as he is tense and concentrated during the game

Princess Anne lends a willing hand

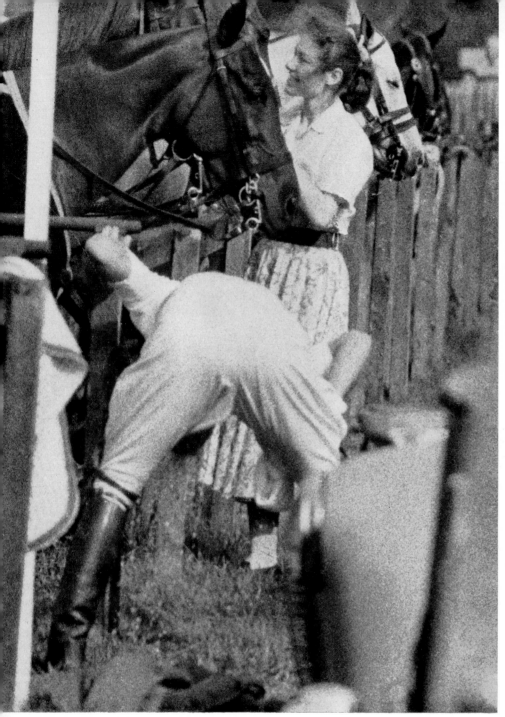

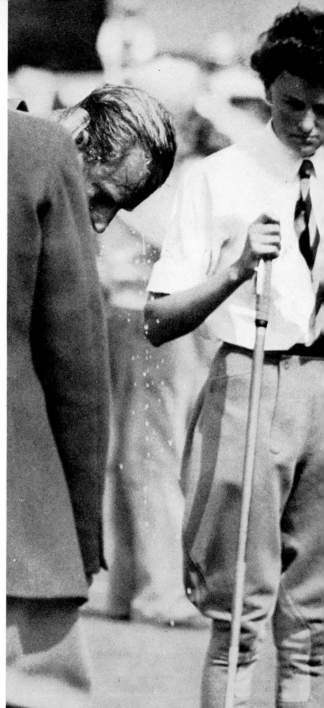

Keeping a watchful eye on polo-playing Prince Philip here is his special detective, Chief Inspector Frank Kelly

advisers at the Court expected of him. He made speeches. He attended premières. He indulged in princely sports. It was not always as easy as he made it seem. Unlike other husbands, he had at all times to strive never to dominate (or even appear to dominate) his wife. He must try to make it plain that he had absolutely no influence over her opinions. Shortly after the Coronation, the Queen – who had taken her husband's name of Mountbatten when she married – reverted to the name of Windsor for herself and her dependants.[1] It was a reminder that she was the senior and most important member of the union, and it might have been unpalatable for Philip to swallow had not the Queen sweetened it with the appointment of her husband as First Gentleman of the Realm.

1. Though Prince Philip, when drawing his family tree for his children, always refers to the family as 'Windsor-Mountbatten'.

34

But was he First Gentleman in fact as well as in title? If he accepted the dicta of the Court advisers, he was certainly not. He knew only too well what they expected of him – no deviation in his attitude from that adopted by Prince Albert, Victoria's Consort, who wrote of his own place in the royal *ménage*:

> 'The position of the Prince Consort requires that the husband should entirely sink his own individual existence in that of his wife; that he should aim at no power by himself or for himself; should shun all attention, assume no separate responsibility, but make his position entirely a part of hers, fill up every gap which as a woman she would naturally leave in the exercise of her regal functions.'

It was a dictum which could have aroused in Prince Philip nothing but feelings of intense frustration. For how was he to interpret it? Did it mean that he must spend the rest of his life acting as a deferential attendant, a pacemaker at receptions, holding up the line with chatty conversation while the Queen got a breather?

For a time, at least, so long as the old guard held sway, that was what was expected of him. With great devotion he dedicated himself to the task of playing second fiddle to the Queen. He was always a step behind her during official visits, a faithful attendant wherever she went, ready to come to her aid and comfort with a word or a touch of his hand. Even when he made a speech on his own he was careful to be discreet, deferential, self-effacing. For one who was anything but self-effacing in fact, who was already bubbling with ideas for modernising the Monarchy, he must have seethed sometimes at the protocol to which he was expected to adhere. He took out his frustration on his polo ponies, on his new cars – which he would drive at over a hundred miles an hour across Windsor Great Park – and on the staffs of the royal residences.

There were unconventional activities in which he could engage so long as they were behind the scenes, and these he did with galvanic energy. As Ranger of Windsor Castle (his first appointment by the Queen) he initiated a plan for putting the estates on a paying basis. He streamlined working methods. He ordered that the vegetables grown in the royal gardens should be sent to market. He started a mushroom farm.

At Buckingham Palace he decided to put more variety into the diet and dispatched Ronald Aubrey, the royal chef, to Paris to learn how to cook Continental dishes.[1] He took to preparing breakfast for himself and the Queen in their bedroom with his own electric frying pan, because it had a habit of arriving lukewarm from the distant kitchens.

It was soon apparent, however, that even if these domestic chores filled his days, they by no means fulfilled his ambitions. He was often bored to distraction by his official routine. He solaced himself by going off to parties with his aide, a friendly Australian named Michael Parker, or on trips to Germany to relax with his favourite sister, Sophie. It was a period of great strain for Prince Philip (and perhaps even more for the Queen) and it manifested itself in outbursts of irritation in public; and since these fits of spleen were often directed against photographers covering royal occasions,[2] they got rather less sympathy and understanding than they deserved.

Fortunately, at least one person correctly diagnosed the reasons behind this nervous tension. The Queen not only sympathised and understood but she also decided to do something to rectify the situation. It was through her intervention that the fundamental change in the nature of Prince Philip's role in regal business came about, and it was a remarkable one. She summoned her advisers. Henceforth, she ordained, Prince Philip would no longer play the part of second fiddle in the royal orchestra. She had decided to make him first trumpet instead. Prince Albert must have turned over in his grave.

She told her advisers to give him an increasing amount of official and public work on his own, without her presence to take away the limelight. In 1952 he was appointed Regent in the event of her death before the majority of the Prince of Wales. In 1956 he departed on an official foreign tour of his own. It was a tour of the Commonwealth which took him around the world in 145 days. It was an enormous success and Philip loved every moment of it.

Neither he nor the fretting *éminences grises* at the Palace remained unaware of the great significance of that tour.

A process had begun. He was stepping out of the Queen's shadow into a limelight of his own. Now he really was First Gentleman of the Realm.

1. Though some months later, paradoxically enough, he complained that he couldn't get any plain English cooking from the royal kitchens.
2. He doused a number of photographers with water at a Chelsea Flower Show, swore at others during a polo match, and pelted still more with peanuts while feeding the monkeys at Gibraltar. The photographers were direfully offended.

'Psst! Keep that —— thing out of his reach until we've got our pictures'

The Royal Family have always been the target for the gentle darts of that splendid observer of the ridiculous, Carl Giles, cartoonist of the *Sunday* and *Daily Express*. The cartoon above is a reference to the incident in 1959 when Prince Philip 'accidentally' sprayed news-cameramen with water from a hose while visiting the Chelsea Flower Show

When Prince Philip began his world tour in 1956 certain foreign newspapers (particularly in Germany) printed rumours that the trip had been organised to give the Queen and her exuberant young husband a chance to breathe separate air for a time. If it was meant to infer that the strain which the Queen's husband was feeling extended to his private life, it was a gross misreading of the situation. In any case, royal trips of such extent and importance are not arranged to settle family tiffs – the Buckingham Palace machine does not work that way.

What is indubitable is the quite considerable emotional gap which both of them felt while the separation lasted, and an animated domestic correspondence failed to bridge it with anything like satisfaction. The Queen let it be known that she was extremely lonely and longed to see her husband again.

Philip had grown a beard during his travels, and news was conveyed to him that

When cameramen pressed him too closely while he was sailing at Cowes, Prince Philip climbed into a motor-boat with Prince Charles and raced across to tell them exactly what he thought of them. Here is Haswell's picture of the incident and, opposite, two versions by *Daily Express* cartoonist Giles of what might have happened

while Prince Charles was looking forward to seizing and tugging it, the Queen and Princess Anne hoped it would be shaved off before he reached home.[1]

It was a maturer, happier and much more integrated Philip who returned from his tour of the world. He exuded a new air of authority and self-confidence, and it was a quality of command which did not go unnoticed among those who hoped to

---

1. It was. But the Queen inspired her family to play a practical joke on Philip of a kind he might have thought up himself. They gave him a private homecoming party at which they all, the Queen included, greeted him wearing false beards.

'I know he don't like you taking his picture while he's racing – but I didn't know he'd
got a polo mallet on board'

'So much for your ''Let's cut across his bows and get our picture in all the papers'' '

'If ever I lay hands on that little —— who said he saw 'em take this road . . .'

The efforts of Prince Philip to conceal the venue to which he took his son, Prince Charles, for his first 'shoot' caused Fleet Street to take out their Ordnance Survey maps and attempt to track him. This is how Giles saw their efforts

benefit from the patronage of royalty. There were always those who hoped that *Philip can influence the Queen, the Queen can influence the Government, so let us influence Philip*. Now their numbers increased. There were Service types who hoped that his affection for the armed forces would win him over to an increase in estimates for a new plane, a new type of ship or tank. There were the Navy types who hoped that his loyalty to the RN would get him on their side in giving priority to naval needs over the RAF or Army.

40

No one was foolish enough, of course, to make overt approaches or suggestions, but it would be equally stupid to pretend that blandishments were not employed. Without acknowledging them, very calmly, shrewdly and without fuss, they were ignored. If his advisers had realised before that he was immune to pressures, now they had confirmation – and confirmation, too, of a new dynamic in Philip's approach to his job as a working partner in the royal relationship.

His ebullient and charming Australian aide, Michael Parker, departed for other spheres of activity, and no longer did his friendly letters of suggestion and advice (which always began: 'Dear Pippo') come to Prince Philip's attention on the breakfast tray. But before he took leave of his chief, Parker did write one memorandum which may yet have its effect upon royal relations with the outside world.

During the period when Parker had worked for Prince Philip there had been moments when their relationship with the Press – and through them with the public – had been stormy. One of their secretaries put it this way:

Michael Parker is at Prince Philip's side at a social gathering. Behind is the late Arthur Christiansen, then editor of the *Daily Express*

'Sometimes things would start fizzing. It was rather as if someone had opened a champagne bottle at the wrong temperature – with the result that someone else got a cork in his eye.'

Parker suggested to 'dear Pippo' that the time was rapidly approaching when Prince Philip should consider setting up a first-class public relations organisation at the Palace to deal with the problem of how to pump a little warmth into his Cold War relationship with the Press. It would need a completely different approach of a kind which might be summed up in a message which hangs in the directors' room of a great American corporation:

'The question is not how we can prevent our critics from doing us harm, but how we can secure their co-operation in doing both of us good.'

Prince Philip promised to think about it.

It was a period when the staffs at the royal residence were encouraged – or perhaps goaded is the more appropriate word – to an intense activity as he modernised and shaped his organisation. His office at Buckingham Palace was turned into an operations-room, complete with maps and plans and coloured stickers, setting out his movements. He broke through the laws against low-flying over London in order that his helicopter could land and take off from the Palace lawns. Always a push-button fan, he turned his office into a whizz-kid's wonderland of electronically operated doors, windows and blinds; used walkie-talkies to communicate with his secretaries and his family; made much use of tape-recorders; and had a push-button TV set fitted into the Queen's bedroom so that they could watch, and change programmes, from bed.

His cars were among the first to be fitted with radio telephones so that he could call the Queen, or his helicopter, or his planes, while he was driving. He became a time-and-motion man, not only in his determination to speed things up in all phases from the gardens at Windsor to the royal kitchens at the Palace, but also in his daily programme of activity. Each morning began with a swim with Prince Andrew in the Palace swimming pool; each evening with an hour in the gym; and the hours between were timed to minutes.

A modern prince indeed. And one today who possesses a privilege which is even denied to his wife, of accepting his own engagements, of writing his own speeches for most of them. It is a position which could prove dangerously intoxicating; and

If you want to fly a helicopter over London you must follow the line of the River Thames because flying low over the city streets is forbidden. An exception has been made, however, in the case of Prince Philip. In order to allow him to keep up with his engagements, he takes off and lands on the lawn of Buckingham Palace and saves hours of time which otherwise might have been spent tied up in traffic jams. This picture shows his helicopter landing at the palace for the first time

there is no doubt that sometimes Prince Philip is so aware of it that he cannot resist the temptation to press his new-found powers just that much too far.

Does the Queen sigh sometimes when she reads the remarks which Philip made (in 1962) to the President of the Republic of Paraguay:

'It's a pleasant change to be in a country which isn't ruled by its people.'

Does she chafe over his evident contempt for politicians? 'To understand what

43

ministers are saying sometimes,' he remarked in 1960, 'you must buy a gobble-degook dictionary and add an arbitrary ten years to every promise they make.'

Will some wild outsider in Parliament or the Press one of these days accuse him of being an opponent of democracy, a gadfly critic of the parliamentary system? 'I sometimes think,' he once told American correspondents in London, 'that it is a pity the peace of the world is left to politicians, who are a quarrelsome lot.'

The Queen is too wise to worry. She knows that her husband is too wise to go too far or desire to, and much too anxious to solidify the basis on which the throne rests rather than wish to undermine its foundations. His exuberance is sometimes apt to sweep him into extravagant actions or statements, but his discretion is great – as anyone has discovered in royal circles who has tried to break the royal rules rather than the more superficial regal conventions. And he possesses an unexpected

Prince Philip drives Princess Anne and Prince Andrew from Buckingham Palace in 1964

quality which can show itself at moments when those who experience it are least forewarned: humility. Palace officials recall the dinner party during one of the crises with the Russians – about Berlin – when Prince Philip was expatiating on what should be done, what actions he would have the Government take, what he thought about the policy of both Allies and opponents. At the conclusion of his peroration he turned to one of his equerries and asked:

'Don't you think I am right?'

The equerry took a deep breath, and then said:

'If I may say so, your Royal Highness, it is a long time since I have heard such a gross misinterpretation of the situation.'

The Queen clapped her hands and said:

'Oh, how wonderful! Does anyone else want to have a go?'

Prince Philip said, quietly:

'Well, I was only trying to give one man's opinion.'

Ever since he called the *Daily Express* 'a bloody awful newspaper' in Rio de Janeiro in 1962 it has been widely assumed that Prince Philip doesn't hate the Press so much (in spite of what photographers say) as Beaverbrook Newspapers. He has certainly been attacking them for years, in private before he reached his present happy state of independence, in public since. But it would be unfair to Philip to let it be assumed that his critical attitude is simply against one section of the Press, for he quite seriously believes that there is not much right with most other organs of news and opinions, in addition to those controlled by the Beaverbrook combine. American correspondents whom he addressed at a luncheon in London in November 1962 were surprised at his evident aversion towards the British Press as a whole. He thought that the *Daily Express* was 'far too savage' in its attacks upon him.[1] He considered *The Times* to be 'far too stodgy'. He dubbed the *Daily Mirror* 'not quite respectable'. He amazed his transatlantic listeners by saying that his favourite newspaper, and, in his opinion, the best in Britain, was *The Guardian*.

But that was four years ago, when his mood was prickly and he was still feeling

1. This was presumably a reaction to the criticisms by Mr John Gordon, in the *Sunday* and not the *Daily Express*, of royal expenditure.

45

his way. In the intervening period some re-thinking about the British Press has taken place at Buckingham Palace and it has not been without its effect on Prince Philip. He is unlikely to be as naive about newspapers – or newspapermen – as he was then; and it is also unlikely that, from now on, he will make the gaffes which so strongly alienated his potential allies in the earlier years of his marriage. Like film stars and pop stars, he is learning to live with the media of news, publicity and gossip. This does not mean that he has lost any of his exuberance or his lively suspicions, and photographers attending royal occasions at which Prince Philip is the star refuse to believe that their tasks will prove much easier in the future. As one of them ruefully said:

'It's something about these naval types. They can't resist their little jokes – and they have a habit of fogging up your lens at the crucial moment.'

He might take comfort from the fact that not always is the sense of humour directed against cameramen, and not always is it crude or overt. Prince Philip has another gambit which is apt to cause some concern among the royal advisers. After a church service at the place where he and the Queen have been staying (usually Balmoral) the officiating clergyman is invited to dinner with the Royal Family and a film show afterwards. Whenever the visiting cleric is a pussyfoot or a puritan, Philip has the habit of asking for an X film to be shown, in order to have a quiet chuckle over the clergyman's blushes.

But the First Gentleman of the Realm, now secure in his position, well aware of his strength and influence, has mellowed and grown wiser with the years. His power has grown, too, and so has his value to a Britain struggling with the doubts and difficulties of the sixties. As partner of the Queen, and no longer just her reticent Consort, his responsibilities are great. He is learning to use them wisely, discreetly and well. He is a very different being indeed from the awkward, craggy, edgy young man who emerged from obscurity to marry a Queen, and was frightened of answering back when bullied by Princess Margaret. Changed indeed. Except possibly in one thing.

One doubts if he will ever cease to think of the *Daily Express* as anything other than 'a bloody awful newspaper'.

A writer once compared Prince Philip's vocabulary when he is annoyed with someone – usually a photographer – with that of a Billingsgate fish-porter. It may be this common gift for colourful language which persuaded him, in 1960, to make a tour of London's famous fish market. He turned up at the same time as the porters, just before dawn, donned a brown overall (but refused one of Billingsgate's famous hats, on which the men balance trays of fish) and spent the next two hours chatting with the men and poking around among the herrings, Dover soles, skate, cod and conger eels. He didn't appear to be shocked by the language he heard around him – 'but then,' as one of the men put it, 'you'd hardly expect him to be, would you, considering the words he sometimes uses himself'

A Rose by any other name

When Princess Margaret celebrated her twenty-first birthday at Balmoral Castle in 1951, one of the royal guests wrote a verse to enliven the occasion:

> 'Some talk of Cleopatra
>   And some of Helen of Troy,
> Of Mr Frank Sinatra—
>   No, dash it, he's a boy!
> But of all the lovely girls we know
>   There's none that's managed yet
> To be as gay in the middle of the day
>   As Princess Margaret.
>
> She recently was twenty
>   And now she's twenty-one.
> These years are packed with plenty
>   Of things that she has done.
> At home she's just as active
>   As when she goes abroad.
> She always looks attractive—
>   Yes, even when she's bored.'

In the life which she now lives as the third most important 'carrier of the royal can' (as a friend of Prince Philip once called the regal round of duties) the chances are that Princess Margaret is very often bored indeed, especially in the middle of the day. Some of the routine ceremonies which fall to her lot can be painfully tedious. It is a tribute to her talent as an actress and her constant anxiety to give a good performance that rarely does a cameraman catch her face in that expression of frozen immobility which indicates that its wearer is numb with ennui.

The cynic may well say of Princess Margaret that the animation of her expression and the freshness of her smile owe much to the professional guidance of her husband, Lord Snowdon, a photographer himself; and that her tolerance of the cameramen who so often swarm around her is (in contrast with the obvious irritation displayed by Prince Philip) a recognition, via her husband, of the facts of life so far as royal photographs are concerned. No one wants to take them, print them or look at them if they are dull. And they will be dull (or distorted) unless those who take them are allowed to come close and choose their own angles.

The job which Princess Margaret fulfills as part of her obligation to the Queen and the Monarchy is one which she herself would perhaps find difficult to define, and about which there has been something of a struggle behind the scenes. For the Queen and her husband there is really no division between their public and private lives, and little choice or desire that the situation should be otherwise. The Queen is Head of the State and the Commonwealth and her husband is First Gentleman of the Realm, and there is no time for anything else. They are on active service for twenty-four hours of the day, and though they have their moments of relaxation, when it comes to the crunch they have no option but to do, go and say as they are advised by the Government of the day.

But does the same obligation, the same liability for service, apply to the Queen's sister? There are those who say that, in the nature of the monarchical establishment, it must. Princess Margaret also receives a subsidy from the State and is maintained out of the national budget; and she therefore has an obligation to support it in every way requested by the powers-that-be. But there are others, reasonable men too, who maintain that Princess Margaret and her husband are in a very different position indeed from that of the Queen, in that their subsidy is considerably less, their responsibility much more equivocal and their liability to the State much more open to question.

Let us put it this way. If Queen Elizabeth the Second were to say to her Government: 'I eschew my subsidies, I revoke my responsibilities, I wish to become a private person,' then Britain would face a constitutional crisis of enormous magnitude – far greater than that which was experienced after the abdication of Edward the Eighth, a far-from-established King. A split in the marriage of the Queen and her husband would do great damage to the institution of the Monarchy (I need hardly add that these are improbabilities presented only to make clear a point in a discussion). Press and Parliament have sometimes adumbrated the suggestion that a remark by Prince Philip (cf. his attacks on politicians) or a particular appointment by Queen Elizabeth (cf. her personal elevation of the Governor of Rhodesia in 1965, during a political controversy) indicate that they have abandoned their regal impartiality and are interfering with, or influencing, the minds of their subjects on political matters by personal intervention. In fact, except for the odd off-the-record remark by Philip – usually on a non-political if not exactly non-controversial subject – the Royal Consortium acts under orders. The Queen would never try to make an appointment without ministerial approval. She accepts the fact that she is a servant of the State.

Is Princess Margaret one as well? How far does her public life have to encroach upon her private occupations? To what extent is her life mortgaged to public opinion and ministerial control?

Even the general public realises by this time that Princess Margaret is the volatile and impetuous member of the royal establishment, and that her temperament is quite different from that of the Queen. Elizabeth knew from the time she was ten years old that her destiny was to be Queen, and her formative years were conditioned by that fact. By the time she was twelve she had met Prince Philip and begun to suspect that he would be her future Consort. The guide-lines of her life were set out for her from the start for her to follow obediently.

Margaret's life was bound to be different and her outlook (conditioned by her sister's calm acceptance of her destiny) was almost bound to be rebellious. It is the not unusual reaction of princes or princesses who are, but only temporarily – as they well know – next in line to a throne, and then are superseded by the birth of a direct heir. The pages of history are stained with the names of brothers, sisters, uncles or cousins of the King who have translated gnawing resentment over their supersession into murderous plots or open rebellion. In our more civilised times things are different. It would be far-fetched to suggest that Princess Margaret has ever had more than the odd moment of envy of her sister's august position and power, and it is doubtful if she has sighed too deeply over her subordinate position. But any psychiatrist would have been troubled had she shown herself too amenable, too calm, too placid in temperament. They did not have to worry because she was not.

From her early teens she demonstrated that she could be both high-spirited and imperious in a way which sometimes made her appear more regal than the Queen. She worked hard at demonstrating that she, at least, was no mere hanger-on to the Queen's train, but a princess in her own right, and downright royal. At the same time, the rebel in her (which in medieval days might have roused her to strike a blow at the Throne) roused her to strike a blow at royal, British and middle-class convention.

Her sister had married a young man whose chief virtue was not – whatever courtiers might think – that he was a prince but that he was many other things besides of more value: he had good looks and health, he had done well in the Royal Navy, he was obviously in love with his adopted land, and was equally obviously determined to become British through and through. The man with whom Princess Margaret fell in love and determined to marry was (except that he was British by birth) not unlike Philip in his background. In fact, they might have come out of the same oven if not from the same mould. Being slightly older than Philip, Group Captain Townsend's service record was even more heroic and distinguished. He, too, was extremely good-looking and intelligent. As far as Princess Margaret was concerned, he was a prince in everything but blood. What did it matter, since he was so superlative in every other way, that he had once been married to someone else?

The ifs of history are an intriguing if wasteful set of permutations to play with, but sometimes one cannot resist them. If King Edward the Eighth had expressed his desire to make Mrs Simpson his morganatic wife in the moral climate of the 1960s, instead of the smug and respectable thirties, would she have been accepted by the British public and would Edward have retained his throne? Somehow, one doubts it, even in the acquiescent atmosphere of today. But if, in today's mood and set of attitudes, Princess Margaret had insisted that she was going to marry Group Captain Townsend, despite his divorced wife, otherwise untainted by scandal, would the advisers at the Palace have stood out against it, and would the public have disapproved?

It seems most unlikely – especially since (even at the time) the Queen Mother is believed to have strongly approved of Townsend and been in favour of the match. Looking back on the affair, it seems almost incredible that Palace censoriousness could have succeeded as effectively as it did in bringing the romance to an end. The irony of it is not much alleviated by the old-fashioned remark, often heard in royal circles:

'Ah well, it all turned out for the best.'

The point which occurs to many people (and no doubt has occurred to Princess Margaret in the intervening years) is: What difference would it have made to the Monarchy, to Britain, to the so-called Establishment, if she *had* married a divorced but otherwise eminently worthy man? One of these days the full story of this sad, sabotaged royal romance will be told in all its Ruritanian detail, and then one surprising fact is likely to emerge: that it was not Princess Margaret's elders who disapproved so strongly as the younger influences at the Palace.

It all seems so long ago. The only reason for its resuscitation here is to indicate the elements which may well have influenced Princess Margaret's attitude towards her royal tasks. It would hardly have been unexpected for her to have adopted a most cynical view of a system which asks of her an unquestioning obedience to the demands of the royal treadmill, but gives her in return none of the rewards of power and proclaim which are the perquisites of the Monarch herself. One might forgive her for saying, in the circumstances: *Dedication is not enough. I must have my own life too.*

Nothing more clearly illustrates Princess Margaret's dilemma than her tour of the United States in the autumn of 1965. It would seem to most reasonable people that it should be part of the education of all members of the Royal Family to have a working knowledge, wherever possible, of all the major countries with which Britain desires to maintain and foster good relations; and that nothing but good could come of a voyage of discovery of the kind which Princess Margaret and Lord

Snowdon made to America in 1965. But this is where the equivocal nature of Princess Margaret's position comes to the fore – and causes criticism in the Press, furore in the House of Commons, and intense distress at Buckingham Palace.

The tour was, in fact, a tremendous success in the United States and received widespread publicity and acclaim. But in Britain itself there was either sour comment or silence. Those who chose to shake their heads but keep their mouths shut did not, of course, include Mr John Gordon, who, like a sheet of living litmus paper, is apt to turn puce every time he is subjected to a report of royal peregrinations. One sometimes feels that Mr Gordon, who rides in a Rolls-Royce himself, would prefer the Royals to walk or bicycle to their appointments, or at least pay for their own petrol. Princess Margaret's tour was easy meat for him, and in the columns of the *Sunday Express* he let loose, at point-blank range, with both barrels.

He wrote:

'Leaving New York after her holiday frolic among the tinsel princes and princesses of Hollywood, Princess Margaret said: "We hope we can come back again."

'Before the next time comes, I hope I won't be considered discourteous or disloyal if I ask: "Who paid for this fantastic tour?" For fantastic it certainly was.

'Take the transatlantic flight first. The party, including attendants and retainers, numbered 14, including an expensive hairdresser. The entire first-class compartment in the BOAC plane (20 seats) was booked. Full fares paid totalled £6,580. Added to that there was roughly £3,000 for one ton of excess baggage.

'Where did the bill go? Not to Kensington Palace, but to a department of the Foreign Office. Who pays in the end? Well, everyone asked simply passes the buck. Lord Snowdon's secretary said that as he merely accompanied the Princess it was very awkward for him to say anything.

'The hairdresser when asked replied with candour: "You can take it that I did not go free of charge, but you must talk to the Foreign Office about these matters." Which seems to suggest that he expects the Foreign Office to pay.

'Apart from the BOAC plane, a private Andover from the Queen's Flight with a crew of seven flew to the United States to carry the holidaymakers on excursions. Who pays for that? Again no one will say.

'Then there is the Princess's special Hartnell wardrobe, costing, I understand, about £1,500. Who pays for that? The Board of Trade says that I must ask the Foreign Office. The Foreign Office, as always, sits mum.

'I calculate the cost of this trip was something over £22,000. I suggest we ought to be told how much of this colossal holiday bill is being paid by the Princess and her husband – and who pays what they don't.'

Mr Gordon's heavy-footed stamps of indignation may have angered the Queen but hardly surprised her, for he is apt to snort with similar trumpets of outrage over the activities of Prince Philip. She must, however, have been shocked when other cutting criticism began to appear, from both Right and Left. The *Sunday Telegraph*, which belongs to a Tory group normally polite towards royalty, lashed out in an editorial of sufficient sociological interest to be quoted at some length:

'Some day, somewhere,' it began, 'the memoirs of Lord Snowdon will doubtless explain how it came about that Princess Margaret's wish to see the United States as a tourist turned into an expensive, exhaustive and dubiously successful semi-royal tour. It will be known which Minister recommended that public money should be spent on first-class air transport for a party of 14 which included, at least part of the time, a leading London hairdresser. It may be possible, looking back, to judge whether it was good for this country's repute – which was obviously the purpose – or harmful.'

The article continued:

'President Johnson has made his judgment in Washington: he said that the visit, by encouraging people to see America, "has helped to balance our payments problem". Mr Wilson is presumably reserving his until he has seen the bill. Whitehall rumours put it at somewhere between £50,000 and £200,000.[1] We are inclined to doubt the latter figure; for the Andover aircraft and its crew of seven from the Queen's Flight, which carried the party for less than

1. The actual cost was £30,000.

This picture was never used at the time it was taken. It shows Princess Margaret and Lord Snowdon (or Mr Anthony Armstrong-Jones, as he then was) attending a rehearsal of their wedding in Westminster Abbey. Robert Haswell had come to the Abbey to take pictures of the workmen preparing it for the ceremony, and could not resist clicking his camera when he spotted the bride and bridegroom-to-be walking down the aisle. He was at once approached by an official and an undertaking was obtained that the photograph would not be used at the time. A pity – because it turned out to be a charming picture

one-tenth of its 15,000-mile round trip, would have cost a substantial sum merely by standing by in Farnborough.'

And the comment ended:

'To Princess Margaret the public would not grudge a "good time" even if it costs us some dollars. About Lord Snowdon opinion is more reserved. With his profession and his patrons, he is something more than a private person and something less than a royal one. There has emanated from this tour an unmistakable whiff of the expense account, for which the responsibility may lie on the other side as here. The Royal Family on the whole has long succeeded, by the most scrupulous judgment and fastidious taste, in avoiding the kind of ambiguities which marked this visit.'

A slap in the royal eye indeed. It was followed by a concentrated onslaught on the visit from the opposite pole of political opinion. First a whole article attacked the visit in the Left Wing *New Statesman*, and then its editor, Mr Paul Johnson, wrote:

'When [Foreign Secretary Michael] Stewart originally approved the tour, the British Ambassador in Washington drew up the customary working engagements for the Princess. When this programme was relayed to her by the Foreign Office, she sent back what one Minister described as "a series of imperious ultimata", saying that she wasn't having any. She *did* fit in the odd working visit here and there, but the normal routine of a royal tour was dropped on her orders, and it thus became not a royal tour but a tour by royalty. There is some bitterness in FO and Government circles that poor [*sic*] Michael Stewart is being made to carry the can. I think he made an error of judgment, but this can fairly be written down to lack of experience in dealing with royalty.'

And then came a particularly waspish sting:

'Meanwhile, some members of the Government, I hear, feel that the Snowdons ought to be given a straight choice between being royal – with all the duties and obligations this implies – or accepting a strictly private status. I've little doubt that the second would be in the best interests of the royal family as a whole.'

This seems to be both harsh and undeserved. For what 'duties and obligations' do Princess Margaret and her husband not already carry out which are not otherwise handed on to other members of the royal entourage, and what more in the way of visits, openings, speeches, christenings and launches could they possibly perform? In Britain in the nineteen-sixties it is surely not going to be suggested that Lord Snowdon is wasting his time and the nation's by having a job, and one which he seems to do well. Is he expected to give it up and become a permanent ornament at ship launchings and Palace levees?

The Queen and Prince Philip are in a class by themselves. But so far as the other Royals are concerned, the time is possibly approaching when some standard of measurement of regal service should be decided for them, and some allowance be made for their private preoccupations. Meanwhile, Princess Margaret cherishes a sense of grievance which is not a whit lessened by the fact that she can be a particularly autocratic and adamant young woman. In Britain in the sixties it is still possible for a title to get a man into jobs and on to directorates which would otherwise be beyond his talents. In the circumstances it seems harsh and unrealistic to suggest that a young, pretty and extremely intelligent princess should be taken off the payroll because she has been accused of arrogance, extravagance, and has a husband who takes photographs for money. It seems to many hard-headed observers of the royal scene today that the objections of most of Princess Margaret's critics are not so much against her predilections as against the fact that her husband works. She must sometimes feel that it is a greater mark against him than the divorce decree was against Group Captain Townsend. Certainly there is no doubt that there are still those at the Palace who regard Lord Snowdon's profession as either a nuisance or a joke. His early struggles for existence and his early jobs – when he went off on assignments as a photographer for daily newspapers – are still thought of as something to be deplored, and he is sometimes suspected of 'guilt by association' with those parts of Press and publicity most disliked by more susceptible Palace servants.

'As long as Madam appreciates that he's not a Viscount Linley and I'm not an Armstrong-Jones . . .'

Giles's comment on the announcement in 1965 that Lord Snowdon had taken his own pictures of his son, Viscount Linley, and Princess Margaret

This is a pity, for nothing has done more to smooth Princess Margaret's path to maturity than her marriage to Lord Snowdon. There are few people who would deny that, since marriage, she is calmer and more self-contained, more physically attractive, more conscious of her dress, her make-up and appearance, more interested in the world around her. And of those who know her, none would deny that Snowdon has been the teacher and his wife an apt and eager pupil. What is certain is that he is an expert and perceptive photographer and any suggestion that he

60

needed a royal marriage to take him to the top of his profession is unfair. It is certain that he would have got there anyway. His apotheosis has been due not to the coronet on his camera but to an avid and artistic eye, and compared with some of the favourite 'royal photographers' he is years ahead in mood and style. Lord Snowdon is reputed to receive a salary of £7,000 a year from Lord Thomson's *Sunday Times* for his photographic contributions to that newspaper. It is an adequate stipend for someone depending on royal connections to bolster his market value, but it is considerably less than he could and almost certainly would have made had he not married Princess Margaret and been forced to circumscribe his photographic activities.

There seems little doubt that the sour criticisms of Princess Margaret and her husband which sprouted in the autumn of 1965 would never have seen the light of day had the Palace in fact reached some decision about how its representatives should be projected. The overall control of the movements and activities of the Royals is exercised by a committee guided by the Queen's private secretary, Sir Michael Adeane. He is a man of great charm, but he knows as much about public relations as a Hottentot. One sometimes gets the impression that he regards every public appearance by royalty as an operation fraught with possibilities of embarrassment, or even disaster, rather than an event to be welcomed and exploited. Anyone who has tried to make inquiries about royal affairs knows how solidly polite and uncommunicative are Palace officials about anything but routine matters. The phrase: 'We have no comment to make' must have been used more frequently, in answer to quite legitimate inquiries, by Palace officials than by any other servant of a head of a state in the rest of the Western world.

It is almost certainly because Princess Margaret and Lord Snowdon have become aware of the sheer amateurism of Palace and Foreign Office public relations that they recently tried to improve matters – not, however, very successfully. Princess Margaret well knows that some of her early tours were far less successful than they might have been, because her advisers were inept and her own attitude all wrong. During her tour of East Africa her officials seemed more anxious to snub reporters and photographers than secure facilities for them. A crisis was reached

during a stop at the Serengeti Game Reserve where cameramen were prevented even from approaching the bungalow where Margaret had stayed the night. They were also banned from taking pictures of her emerging from the door of the bungalow next morning, an action which caused one photographer to remark, sourly:

'We're not trying to take her picture in bed, we're merely trying to show her coming out after breakfast.'

The result was that, on this tour, so reluctant and unforthcoming was royal co-operation that one photographer, unable to get them together, faked a photograph of Princess Margaret staring into the eyes of a rhinoceros when, in fact, the beauty and the beast were half a mile apart.

Before Lord Snowdon's advent, too, there was always the problem of when Princess Margaret was 'private' and when she was 'public'. Observers recall her

Princess Margaret seemed subdued and rather unhappy at times during her tour of East Africa in 1956. Officialdom was out in force and photographers accompanying the tour found it difficult to get the attractive close-up or unconventional shot for which they are always looking. They had their most disappointing time when the Princess visited the Serengeti Game Park, where they hoped to picture her close to one or other of the herds of game with which the park abounds. But they were never allowed to get near enough. In fact, the scene showing Princess Margaret in close proximity to a rushing rhino was shot through a 'Long Tom' lens. Princess and animal were actually well away from each other, but the effect of the photograph was to bring beauty and the beast together

Princess Margaret during her tour of East Africa in 1956

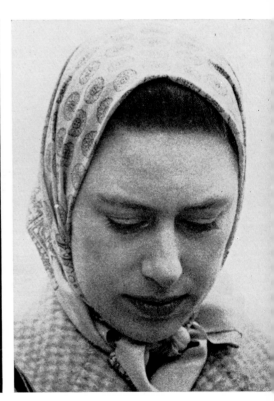

A thought for the card at Epsom in 1957

Pensively at the Badminton Horse Trials

The changing face of Princess Margaret

Depending on the time, the place and the mood, she can look so different, as
these studies taken in various parts of the world by Haswell show

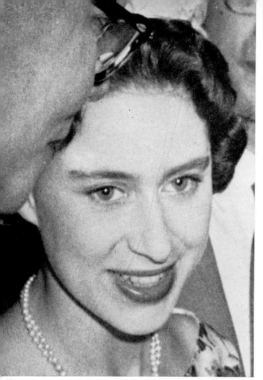

Her successful West Indies tour in 1958 saw her at her most serene

A completely 'different' Margaret at Lancaster
House in 1962

With Lord Snowdon at a Boat Race practice,
obviously happy in spite of the rain

A near miss in Belgium. During a visit to Bruges in 1958 Princess Margaret was walking across the *place* when a car edged its way through the crowd, horn blaring, the driver apparently unaware of the royal visit. Alarmed by the shouts of detectives, the driver finally stamped on his brakes and the car brushed against Princess Margaret's skirt as it slid to a halt. The incident seems to have upset the Princess, and she was intensely nervous for the rest of the day, flinching every time a camera flash went off. Later that day: there is a wariness behind her smile as she walks in the rain

Princess Margaret out for a ride during her visit to Portugal in 1959. The visit was supposed to be private, but Portuguese officials 'leaked' details of her programme, and a horde of international photographers arrived

The secret mission

In 1963, rumours began to be heard around Windsor that Princess Margaret and Lord Snowdon were preparing themselves for 'a secret mission'. No one knew quite what the mission was but the general consensus of opinion (uninformed opinion, that is) was that they were undergoing training for a spectacular underwater exploration project – possibly diving for sunken treasure in the West Indies. What was certain was that, whenever they could take the time off together, they would pack frogmen's kit into their car and take off for an unknown destination. No one could pin down where they went or exactly what they were doing.

A few weeks of intensive detective work by Robert Haswell produced a much less fantastic explanation, plus a series of delightful pictures. Lord Snowdon had decided that his wife should learn to water-ski, and that his own technique could do with some polishing. A water-skiing expert, Barry Connel, was called in, and a disused gravel pit near Reading chosen for the exercise. Only a few close friends were told, so that cameramen should not be on hand to photograph the embarrassing moments.

Haswell got his pictures, anyway. And there were *no* embarrassing moments. Even when she was sinking into the water, Princess Margaret managed to look both beautiful and graceful in her tight-fitting rubber suit; and Lord Snowdon splashed down if not with grace, certainly with élan.

71

Lord Snowdon has several times taken his wife to stay with his mother at Ross Castle, in Eire. This photograph shows him during one of these visits out for a day's shooting. *Left to right:* Mr Billy Wallace, Lord Snowdon, Chief Inspector Crocker

The apartment on the Thames, in dockside London, where Princess Margaret and Lord Snowdon used to meet before their marriage. This famous photograph shows Mr Tony Armstrong-Jones, his bride beside him, waving to his ex-landlord as the newlyweds sail for their honeymoon aboard the Royal Yacht

For formal occasions, Royalty must have a chauffeur, but whenever they can dispense with him – or put him into the passenger seat – the Snowdons like to drive themselves, as these pictures show. (**1**) Lord Snowdon and his chauffeur (safety belts fixed) driving away from Hyde Park Corner (**2**) The Snowdon Rolls-Royce heading for Buckingham Palace, with Margaret signalling a left turn through the window (**3**) Lord Snowdon driving, Princess Margaret beside him, with their chauffeur in the back seat

so-called 'private' visit to Portugal which was preceded by so much word-of-mouth publicity that one might have thought that Greta Garbo was about to dangle one of her 'I want to be alone' carrots before the hungry Press. As a result, British, French, Italian and American newspapers and magazines drafted cameramen and reporters to cover the visit. One English reporter bought for £100, from the Portuguese Ministry of Foreign Affairs, the complete itinerary of her visit, and was therefore always *in situ* when Margaret appeared. Not that it would have been difficult to miss her, since she travelled everywhere with a team of Portuguese motor-cycle police sirening her progress from A to B.

Not unexpectedly, photographers were everywhere and were methodically rooted out by Portuguese police under the superintendence of a Scotland Yard inspector. One of the places chosen by the Princess and her party for a swim was a rich magnate's pool which was overlooked by a small village on the opposite hillside. Hours before the Princess arrived, every household had been invaded by cameramen offering bribes to the amazed Portuguese for vantage points at their bedroom windows. Soon the police were on the scene, and a house-to-house search resulted in cameramen being dragged from under the beds and out of the clothes closets where they had been hiding. At a British Embassy cocktail party that evening a police official boasted that he had quite outwitted the photographers. He had not. A cameraman from *Paris Match* had, fortunately for him, inveigled himself into a house with a loft above the bedroom, and there he had hidden until the search was over – after which he descended to take his pictures. These innocent views of Margaret taking a swim were, as a result of the disturbance, soon being printed all over the world.

In the hope of resolving this guerilla warfare between Princess Margaret's protection squad and the cameramen, Lord Snowdon has attempted to organise some system of his own which might circumvent the clumsiness of Palace officials and ham-handed policemen. It must be admitted that his efforts have so far not been successful, possibly because of the misguided nature of his approach.

To some extent it could be said that the influence of some of his friends in the world of entertainment is to blame for that. Since their marriage, Princess Margaret and her husband have become quite friendly with the English film star, Peter Sellers, and his young Swedish wife, Britt Eklund, and nothing has impressed them more than the manner in which an efficient public relations organisation has coped with the problems of the Sellers regime. Under the direction of a shrewd man named Theo Cowan (who once looked after the personal appearances of film stars working for the Rank Organisation) Sellers and his wife are now confident that they can turn publicity on and off like a tap, and be reasonably sure of the type of image they wish to present to the public. All interviews, statements and public appearances are processed through the Cowan Organisation, and it is no coincidence that they usually take place just before a film or play in which they are appearing is about to be presented. Otherwise, Mr Cowan's task is to preserve the privacy of his clients and to see that nothing is made public about them which they would not wish to see in print.[1]

'Cowan treats his clients like royalty,' is a remark made in film circles, 'and he gets the royal treatment for them.'

For anyone to imagine, however, that the sort of operation which polishes the image of a film star is one likely to give an extra sparkle to a royal tiara is to reveal a basic misunderstanding of Princess Margaret's problem. Film, stage, television and 'pop' stars employ publicity agents because even the most respectable of them are thought to be not quite so by the public which pays money to see them. They figure in divorce suits. They get involved in fights in night clubs. They are creatures of vanity who have to be constantly assured of their superlative qualities. And most of them have achieved, rather too quickly, a station in life for which they have had insufficient training. For them it is a largely fictional rather than a truthful image which the publicity agent projects. His job is less to give out facts than create a myth. To glamorise.

Princess Margaret has no need of such promotion. It is the kind of 'apple polishing', as Madison Avenue calls it, which is more likely to cause her embarrassment than otherwise, as those who talked to her after her first visit to the United States well know. She was saddened and discomfited by the reaction in Britain to her tour, and repeatedly asked:

'Why did it go wrong? What did I do?'

It was not what she did. It was what was done to her.

---

1. Nothing has appeared, for example, of the visits which the Snowdons have made to the Sellers home in Surrey.

It seems particularly unfortunate that the Snowdons, having decided to utilise a publicity organisation for their tour – and that was what they did – failed to make sure that the prime purpose of their journey, to show the flag, to boost British goods, was kept to the fore. Perhaps the most serious mistake was to allow an old friend of Princess Margaret, Miss Sharman Douglas, to act as 'front' man for the journey and allow her, in her charming and misguided way, to pervert the whole purpose of the tour. To the motto on the wall which says: 'Never let your husband teach you how to drive' should be added one saying: 'Never let your best friend be your agent.' Miss Douglas devoted most of her attention to seeing that Princess Margaret met 'all the most glamorous and interesting people' and 'really had herself a ball'. But that isn't what royal visits are for. Royal visits are to allow ordinary people to see royalty and get some idea of what hard-working, pleasant and inquiring people they are. There is no doubt that the American people enjoyed what they saw of the Snowdons, but there is also no doubt that thanks to Miss Douglas's misguided enterprise the British people got the impression that the whole thing was an expensive junket – party after party – and that the Princess never got anywhere near the real American people.

If Princess Margaret was the problem-child of the Royals before, the acrimony provoked by her US visit has certainly exacerbated the situation. She must now be tempted to do just what her critics suggest, and retire to private life. She will probably resist it because, as she frankly admits, she likes her life as a royal princess. But even if she did not, it is most unlikely that the Queen would allow her to withdraw into the background, at least until her own daughter, Princess Anne, is older and able to take part in the royal round of duties.

Meanwhile, Margaret is direfully in need of someone who can correct the misconceptions about her, and show that her life is far from being an imperious peregrination from party to party, and that hobnobbing with film stars, listening to jazz and looking beautiful is far from being the sum total of her talents. It seems extraordinary that a young woman of her looks, charm and brains should attract such rancour from her critics, and that she should lack a champion.

Had she the freedom possessed by her brother-in-law, Prince Philip, to speak out in public, there is little doubt that she too might gain a reputation for frankness and controversy; and those who now infer that she is a feather-brain would discover that her opinions are forthright, her outlook is sometimes disconcertingly modern, and that she has little time at all for any kind of privilege not earned by constant attention to the job.

One of Margaret's grievances is that too often the picture seen of her is one in which she is wearing a tiara and a low-cut evening gown as she sweeps into a film première or a musical, and she can almost hear the remark at the nation's breakfast table next morning:

'I see that Margaret's had another night out.'

There is no opportunity of explaining that the 'night out' (which might well be the première of a play or film she doesn't particularly want to see) has come at the end of a gruelling day during which she has risen at six, flown to Cornwall, opened a hospital wing, reviewed some cadets, launched a ship and spoken to old age pensioners. She has had to memorise a speech plus a long list of names of officials; she has had only a couple of hours in which to take a bath, have her hair done, get dressed and snatch a gin-and-tonic before setting out for the theatre.

Since Lord Snowdon has a job of his own, she is continually discovering that her day off is his day on, and that sometimes nearly a week can go by without their having more than a snatched breakfast together. She often discovers that her official duties bring her into longer contact with other people's children than her own. Yet she is a devoted mother, constantly watching her offspring for signs of showing off, always reminding their governess not to pamper them, reminding them constantly that they mustn't be rude, especially to servants, since they will grow up to be servants themselves. She is firmly of the opinion that some royal children have been encouraged to be self-important and superior, and any such instincts she detects in her own are put down with a brisk, no-nonsense-from-you attitude which is refreshing to watch.

Undoubtedly she is the most modern-minded member of the Royals, and her witty tongue can sometimes get her into trouble. There were some officials at the Palace, for instance, who were not amused when the Beatles were made MBEs (or Members of the Order of the British Empire) and she suggested that the letters stood for 'Meant for Brian Epstein'. She is known to have scandalised a dinner table attended by members of the Church by ridiculing 'with it' bishops who acted like 'pop' stars. Once when Richard Burton was reported as having described his

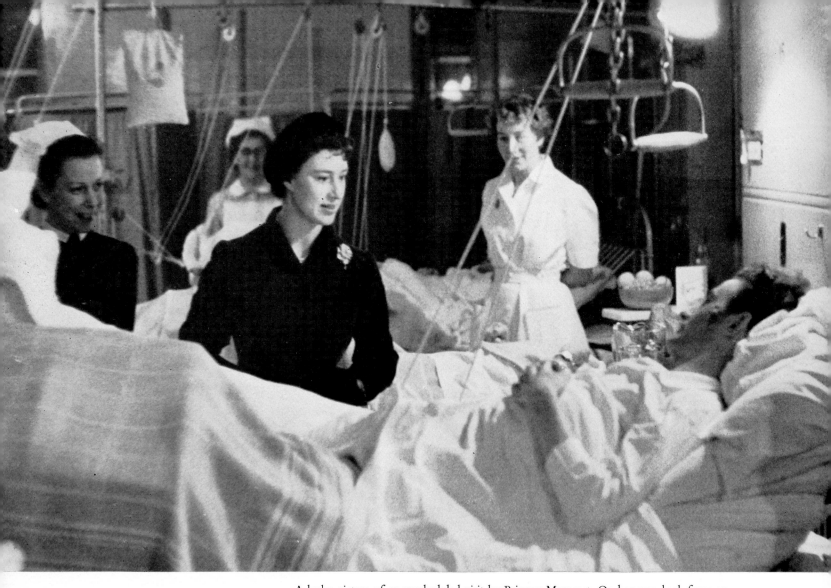

A lucky picture of an unscheduled visit by Princess Margaret. On her way back from an official tour she decided to stop off at the hospital where victims of a big rail crash had been taken. Haswell, unaware of her plan, drove up to the hospital at almost the same time and heard Margaret's detective whisper: 'He must be clairvoyant!'

wife's legs as 'dumpy' she froze a couple of middle-aged aldermen by saying: 'He should see mine.' Unlike Queen Victoria, who considered that even piano legs should be covered, she sees no reason to conceal the fact that royal personages have the same kind of bodies and feel the same needs and emotions as the rest of mankind.

For Princess Margaret, the problem of the future – and the worry of the Queen – is how she can continue to play her part in the business of royalty ('damned hard work – but it's wonderful when you know you're looking nice and they start to cheer') and still share her life with her husband and children, still go off when she

82

feels the need of a break from routine and still enjoy the exuberant and often unconventional private life which is so frowned upon by the staider members of the royal entourage.

'Oh, for a life where I could sometimes dye my hair another colour, or go for a swim in the nude!' she was once heard to say. The revelations of the Profumo scandal, far from making her eyes pop out with horrified shock, made them sparkle with wry amusement at the fallibilities of mankind; and from 'op' art through electronic music, kitchen-sink drama, sex-films and gruesome murder trials, there is very little nowadays which she doesn't want to know about. It is said that she once thought an amusing dinner party would be one at which she was the hostess and the other guests were Malcolm Muggeridge, Mick Jagger, David Hockney, Elizabeth Taylor, Nell Dunn, Edna O'Brien, the Lord Chief Justice and John Gordon. It would have made quite an evening.

She has a lively mind, and her marriage to Lord Snowdon, and the consequent widening of her horizons, has helped to keep it malleable and avid for more information and experience. How long she can reconcile this thirst for new ideas and places with the day-to-day business of being a deputy for the Queen is one of the more fascinating talking points in royal circles today. But one thing is certain. She will stay and do the job just as long as the Queen needs her.

Whenever Royalty goes abroad, their special detectives go with them: to liaise with the local police over protection measures, to watch out for the unexpected incident, to keep crowds and photographers at a distance. Here is Chief Inspector Fred Crocker who used to look after Princess Margaret

Bringing up Charles, et cetera

One afternoon at Smith's Lawn, Windsor, when the Royal Family had gathered to watch Prince Philip playing polo, the Queen turned to her son and asked him to call her bodyguard, Inspector Perkins.

Prince Charles sauntered over to the corner of the tent in which they were sitting and called out, loudly:

'Perkins! You're wanted!'

Those who saw the expression on the Queen's face as she heard him are convinced that when the Prince of Wales returned to Windsor Castle he got the wigging of his life; for she was obviously outraged at the arrogant impudence of a young boy so rudely addressing an official of Perkins' standing and maturity. So far as the Queen is concerned, not even a tweeny at the Palace is treated like a lackey, and impoliteness pains her, especially when it is directed at someone who cannot answer back.

It is no secret that the moulding of Prince Charles's character is one of the problems which most concerns the Queen, and one strongly suspects that her ideas of how it should be done do not always coincide with those of Prince Philip. Not unnaturally, as any father would, he has encouraged the Prince of Wales to emulate his own activities and outlook in the conviction that such are the makings of a man. But whether they are also the makings of a future King of England and Head of the Commonwealth is something else again. Most sons who are proud of their fathers (as Charles undoubtedly is of Prince Philip) hope for nothing better than to follow in their footsteps. It is something the Prince of Wales will never do, for Prince Philip is but the husband of the Queen, while his son was born and destined to be King – a very different position and one requiring an altogether different approach to the responsibilities he will one day be confronting.

It is, of course, only to be expected that Prince Philip should be intensely anxious to make his son as tough and as durable as he is himself, for these were the qualities which enabled him to survive the rigours and unhappiness of his own childhood. When measuring his character and assessing his attitudes, the formative influences of his childhood should constantly be borne in mind, and they explain a good deal about his attitude towards his son. While still almost a baby, he had to flee the country of his birth; and during his early boyhood he was deprived of that fundamental need – a stable and happy parental environment. His father and mother, Prince Andrew and Princess Alice, lived apart; he was shuttled back and forth between relations; for a time he didn't know whether he was going to grow up a little German or a little Englishman; and he learned that a bold front, a certain pugnacity, a protective armour of remoteness were the qualities which sustained him through the lonelier moments.

It is a training which has shaped Prince Philip into the brilliant, hard-driving, craggy, self-contained man he is today. It is a training which has also shaped many of the leaders whom he meets, who have also fought their way through from obscurity or through adversity to the top: millionaires, trade union leaders, ministers, presidents and commissars. He can talk to them on equal terms and argue with them if he does not agree with what they are saying; he has earned the right, and he is not speaking for anyone but himself.

The circumstances of the Prince of Wales are, however, so different that he surely does not have to marinate himself in the same vinegar as that which hardened and toughened his father. His family life has been stable and happy, his future assured; and with a lesson from Greece before them of what trouble can result when a young King is wilful, dictatorial or implacable, those who share the task of educating the heir to the throne are concerned to make sure that Prince Charles grows up to be a man and a King, but never forgets that he is a servant of his Governments and his peoples.

One of their problems is that Prince Charles yearns to be like his father in every

Prince Charles off to a shoot in Sussex, 1960

way, and with the recklessness and exaggeration of youth, is inclined to emulate him even in his occasional indiscretions. He and his sister, Princess Anne, have heard their father say:

'I'll admit I'm bloody nasty to the photographer who pokes his long lens through the keyhole into my private life. I'll never be rude to the photographer who is doing his job. But I will be if my privacy is invaded.'

Their reaction has been to resent photographers on all occasions, including lawful ones. When Prince Charles was out in a speedboat he spotted photographers on the shore and sped towards them, swerving just before he reached them, whether to give them a close-up or to inundate them and their cameras with the wash from

'Planned like a commando raid' . . . a well-escorted Prince Charles sets out for a shooting session. *Above:* That Giles cartoon again

89

his boat is a matter of speculation. Neither he nor Princess Anne seem able to resist pulling faces at the cameramen; though this is a tendency which the Princess, like any other pretty girl, will undoubtedly grow out of as she learns from seeing her picture in the papers that a photographer can be her kindest friend and unpleasantest critic.

But of course it is not just in his mild prejudices that the Prince of Wales wants to emulate his father. There was a time when the only game he played was table-tennis because it was the one game, he said, over which his father didn't bully him to do better. He was apt to be timid. When Prince Philip, whose fondness for the sea is not simply the result of his naval training, used to take him out in a small boat, Prince Charles hated every moment of it. (He still doesn't really like being on the water.) For a time it could be said that his younger brother, Prince Andrew, was his father's favourite son, and the knowledge of it obviously roused Charles to show his mettle.

Gordonstoun was the great challenge, for there his father's successful example was always before him.

'When Philip came to Gordonstoun,' its famous headmaster, Dr Hahn, wrote, 'his most marked trait was his undefeatable spirit. He felt the emotions of both joy and sadness deeply, and the way he looked and the way he moved indicated what he felt. That even applied to the minor disappointments in a schoolboy's life. His laughter was heard everywhere. He had inherited from his Danish family the capacity to derive great fun from small incidents. In his school work he showed a lively intelligence. In community life, once he made a task his own, he showed meticulous attention to detail and pride of workmanship which was never content with mediocre results.'

And later Hahn wrote:

'Prince Philip is a born leader, but he will need the exacting demands of a great service to do justice to himself.'

As he woke up and marched through the grey dawn to a cold shower on the morning of his first day at Gordonstoun, Prince Charles must have been a very lonely boy, and possibly a frightened one too, especially since every other boy in the school – and all the masters – must have been looking at him, and wondering.

Some public schools might have bent their rules to accommodate a future King, but not Gordonstoun, and the first term for Prince Charles was a salutary experience about which, no doubt, we will hear more one day. But when he returned after his first holiday a metamorphosis had taken place and there was a zest and a determination to succeed which was at once noticeable to everyone in the school. One gets a glimpse of how it started so ill and finished so well from a story told to me by a young Ethiopian prince, the Duke of Harar, who may well one day be an Emperor himself. This dark-skinned, handsome boy from the uplands of Africa came to Gordonstoun a couple of years after Prince Charles, and on his first morning was gazing through the rain at the alien Scottish landscape and feeling 'not very good', as he put it.

An older boy came up to him. 'What's your name?' he asked, and the Duke told him. 'Cheer up!' he said. 'The first weeks are absolute murder and you want to cut your throat. But after that it's smashing!' It was, of course, Prince Charles.

Gordonstoun gave the Prince of Wales confidence, and lost him the shyness and sense of inadequacy he had hitherto felt in the presence of his father. It was he who suggested to Prince Philip that he should be allowed to play polo, and he quickly demonstrated a thrusting eagerness that forced his delighted father to suggest that he was being a little too reckless for a beginner. When he had achieved some confidence, word was leaked that he would be on view at a public game and the photographers were invited to come along. It was one occasion when he welcomed rather than resented them, and was too busy squinting at the ball to pull faces at the camera.

The cameramen were less welcome when Prince Philip for the first time took the Prince of Wales shooting with him. It is one of the sports which he is anxious not to have publicised, since he believes that the British public is extremely sensitive – he might have used the word hypocritical – when it comes to shooting birds or animals for the table. They do not seem to object to the sight of pheasants, partridges, grouse and duck hanging in the butchers' windows, and they eat them with relish when they can afford them, but they appear to be revolted by the fact that someone had to shoot them first. As a result, Prince Philip, who likes deer-stalking,

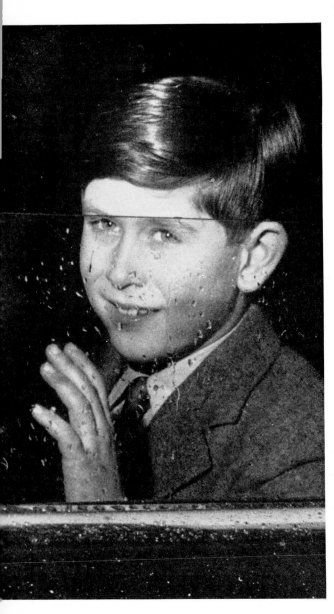

Prince Charles rarely pauses to pose for photographers, for whom he sometimes seems to share his father's antipathy. So most shots of him are apt to be unconventional. These two are exceptional: He is on his way to Buckingham Palace from school; he rides at Badminton

Prince Charles stamping down the turf on the polo ground where his father was playing in Windsor Great Park. Bored, he lets the water out of the rain-soaked marquee during a rainstorm at Windsor

It was in 1963 that Prince Charles started learning to ski in earnest. He chose the nursery slopes at Schuls, in Switzerland, and after some preliminary spills proved to be an apt pupil. In between practice sessions, he toured the town by sleigh with a friend, Prince Carl of Germany

One day in 1964 word reached Fleet Street from sources at Buckingham Palace that photographers attending the weekend polo game at Smith's Lawn, Windsor Great Park, might find something of more than ordinary interest. They certainly did. In the gym at Buckingham Palace and secretly at Windsor the Prince of Wales and Prince Philip had been practising polo together. Now Prince Charles was considered skilful enough to demonstrate his prowess in public, and a cheer went up from the spectators as he cantered on to the field behind his father. He played a game which may have lacked Prince Philip's skill, but showed the same boldness and determination. Friends say he fully shares his father's enthusiasm for polo. The same can hardly be said for sailing, another of Prince Philip's hobbies and one which Prince Charles dislikes

hawking and game-shooting, prefers to keep these activities as secret as a military operation when he indulges in them. His first outing with his son was planned like a commando raid and an attempt was made to cut off all private roads and paths leading to the countryside where the shoot was to take place. Inevitably the photographers, armed with ordnance survey maps, found public footpaths through and were on hand when father and son, guns on shoulders, walked past, the expressions on their faces anything but welcome on this occasion.

Since that time the Prince of Wales has become a keen gunman. He and his father have started an ornate illuminated gunroom, bedecked with their trophies, at Sandringham, and the Prince of Wales longs for the day when he has the same expensive Purdy guns as his father, with a gold inlayed 'C' where Philip has 'P'.

Every mother watches father and son as they grow and develop together, and the Queen is no exception in this; and no exception in pondering whether the young man being groomed, the character being formed, is one which, aside from maternal love and regard, she can approve. The Queen must remember at all times that this son of hers will one day take her place at the head of the Commonwealth and be worthy of kingship. Does he have the capacity, the dedication, the sense of purpose, the – above all – humility?

There are the more practical, but equally important, matters too. Who will be his wife?

It seems to have escaped the notice of most people who write criticising the Royal Family and speculating on the future of the Monarchy that, in a year or two, the future King of England will fall in love and take a bride, though the two events will not necessarily coincide in time nor concern the same person. It would be cosy and comforting to believe that, when the time comes, the Prince of Wales will meet the girl of his choice, adore her to distraction, and make her Queen of England. It seems doubtful. The last time a Prince of Wales tried it, disaster.

Though moral values have changed, standards are different, attitudes are awry, it still seems more than likely that the bride of the Prince of Wales will be chosen for him rather than picked by him, and that the pulse-beat of national interest rather than the heart-beat of passion will decide the choice. But who will it be? Or rather, what kind of bride will the British public be persuaded to take to their hearts?

It seems unlikely that, by this time, the eligible daughters of the fading European princelings will any longer be considered worthy even if eligible to occupy the throne of England. Prince Philip's sisters in Germany have no less than fifteen eligible daughters and sons waiting to be married off, but they are in too close consanguinity to be considered.

One hopes that what Prince Philip and the Queen agree upon is not – for it is impossible – a free choice by their son of his bride-to-be, but of a width of choice which will engage the sympathy and understanding of the public once the decision is made. It has developed into a world in which a future King of England must needs look beyond the remnants of European royalty, the daughters of British aristocracy, for a young woman of sufficient beauty, talent and dedication to share a throne with a King of England in the shaky but exciting decades to come.

No one at the Palace would deny that a radical change in the attitude towards royal marriage is taking place at the moment, and that the time may well have come when an heir to the British throne looks rather to the Commonwealth than to the draughty palaces of Europe for the young woman who will be his bride, and his Queen. One wonders whether she will be Canadian or Australian.

If one talks to the parents whose daughters go to Benenden, one gets the impression that here, too, is a school which believes that a pampered child is a poor risk, and that rigid discipline may not make for happy children but certainly keeps them in order. Since the Queen's daughter joined there are some pupils who suggest that regulations have been tightened to turn it into a feminine Gordonstoun, and they have dubbed it Annesville. Others, however, as stoutly maintain that it hasn't changed a whit.

This may be because Princess Anne has that sort of personality which appears to penetrate the armour of indifference usually adopted by the seniors at a girls' school towards those who have just entered as juniors, and that her sturdy and adamant attitude towards her seniors has made itself felt. She is a girl whose *persona* is apt to arouse feelings which, either pro or con, are certainly strong. Not long ago Mr Henry Fairlie wrote in *Encounter*:[1]

1. October 1961.

'I have a friend who cannot bear the sight of Princess Anne. Although he is otherwise a self-controlled person, a photograph of her, especially if she is giving that condescending little wave, or stir, which has become one of the inherited graces of the British Royal Family, moves him to a hysterical rage. I have known him to spread out on the floor in his office every morning newspaper which carried a picture of her, and even send out his secretary for more, in order to feed his consuming indignation. I have seen his fingers quiver as he points at her haircut, his lips go pale as he rails at her coat, or her hat, even at her shoes.'

One wonders what potent projection of a particular kind Princess Anne must possess that she should arouse such a fervour of antipathy, since she was only eleven years old at the time, and the spokesman for these strong feelings does not even appear to have met her.

The problem of Princess Anne's future in the royal heirarchy is by no means as urgent as that of her brother, for he will be King and she will be – what? If a parallel is to be drawn between her position as sister of the Prince of Wales and that of two generations back, when Prince Edward was heir to the throne and Princess Mary his sister, one can only hope that her talents and potentialities will not be mortgaged quite so quickly.

From what one gathers of her forthright character and her eagerness to engage in the life of her country, possibly in some service overseas, one doubts if Princess Anne will succumb too quickly to the pressures of those who might wish to marry her off to a rich sprig of the aristocracy or a European cousin. Nothing has aroused more talk at Benenden[1] than the sturdy refusal by the Dutch royal princesses to have their future spouses chosen for them either by their family or by the Government, and it is almost certain that the implications for herself have not passed her by.

One cherishes a certain sympathy for the young man, suing for her favours, who will have the job of winning over Prince Philip, for one senses that he will prove to be a potential father-in-law more hypercritical of possible candidates than most. The Queen, on the other hand, is likely to be at the same time blander and kindlier while much firmer and more determined in her judgment. Not that either of them are likely to swerve Princess Anne once she has made up her mind. The Prince of

1. Except, possibly, the raid on the school by some male students from Croydon.

Wales will marry the bride who is hand-picked for him. His sister is likely to be the first daughter of a reigning monarch to be able – if she insists, as she likely will – to choose her own spouse. Or even her own way of life.

Five years in the life of a young girl can make all the difference, as these photographs show. The uncomplicated tot in the striped dress, obviously much more interested in the horses than the cameramen, was Princess Anne at Windsor Great Park in 1959, where her father was playing polo.

She was a year older, and possibly aware that she had grown just a little plump, when she was photographed in corduroy slacks and sweater at another of her father's matches; though she had slimmed down a few months later when she went with her family to the horse show at Badminton. By 1962, though she lolls easily atop a jeep, she seems to be quite aware that she is growing up fast and is very happy about it.

Then in 1963, at Benenden, she seems to be facing, for the first time, the fact that she has left childhood behind her for good; and it is a serious moment. And finally, back to Windsor again. The same occasion—a polo match. The same ponies. But a grown-up and attractive young woman now, poised, aware – and a world away in experience from the finger-sucking child of 1959

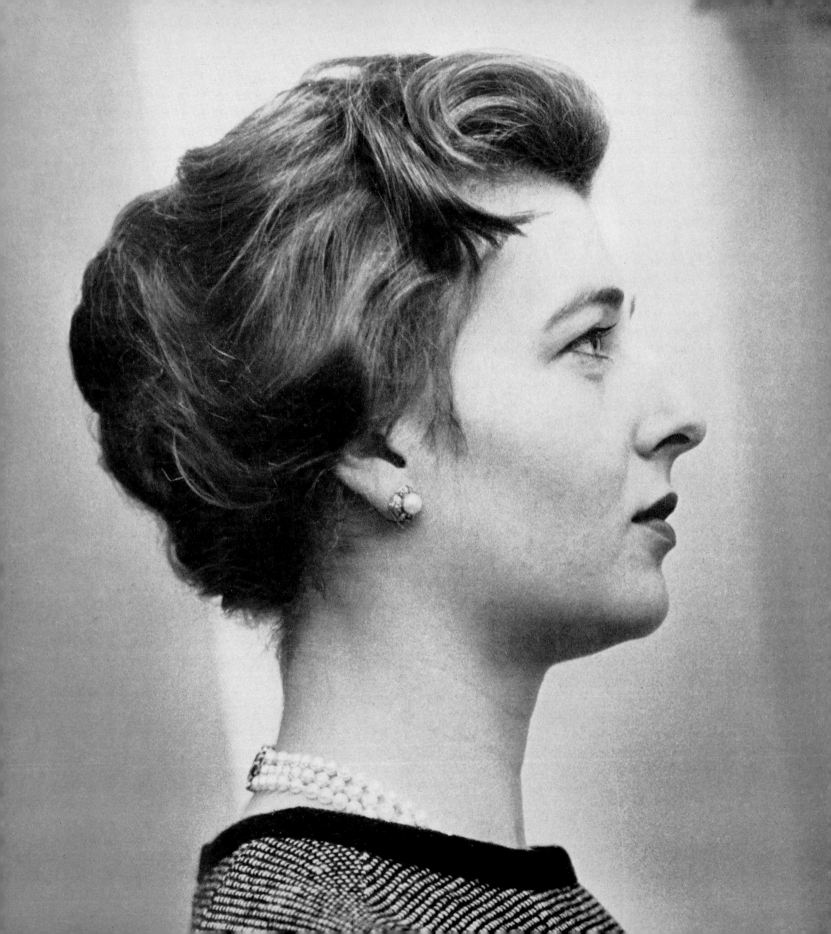

She also serves

One evening, as she travelled back from her fourth visit to a shipyard in a month, Princess Alexandra said:

'They should call me Helen of Troy. Wasn't she the girl who launched a thousand ships?'

For several years now Alexandra has been fourth in line, after the Queen, Prince Philip and Princess Margaret, as the carrier-out of royal chores and routines, and despite the happy look on her face in the pictures in the newspapers she does not enjoy all of them. She is well aware that several of the openings and factory tours which she indefatigably performs are those which have been rejected by her cousin Margaret as being too dull, too messy or too trivial. She has been known to remark, wryly, as she drives away from yet another hospital ward or old folks' home:

'They'd much rather have had Elizabeth Taylor – or some TV star. But film stars only come when they've got a new film to publicise. And the TV people all charge fees, these days, I hear. Ah well, I may not be as pretty as Mick Jagger, but at least I'm free!'

Alexandra does herself an injustice. If she did charge a fee, like 'pop' stars and sports idols, they would almost certainly still ask her, and her 'take' would be considerable. For it is extraordinary how frequently she manages to get an event of infinite unimportance into the newspapers and the TV newsreels, all because of the pleasantly potent quality of her personality and the photogenic character of her features. Plus the fact that cameramen adore her.

Those who smile at the easy-going, spontaneous self-confidence which Alexandra nowadays displays whenever she moves around in public, and think of her as the most exuberantly natural of all the Royals, don't realise that it took hard work behind the scenes to make her that way – and a domestic crisis at the Palace to get her into the front rank of the royal line-up at all.

For the successful projection she owes much to the skilful planning and manipulating of two people who have always been ambitious for her: her mother, Princess Marina, and the comptroller of Marina's household, Sir Philip Hay.

Princess Marina once had an offer from an international public relations set-up with some awesome clients, a couple of presidents among them, to join the organisation as an adviser on how to deal with, present and project their more distinguished customers. The fees offered would have solved many of her pressing problems, for the allowance which was being made to her by the Royal Family after the death of her husband, the Duke of Kent, was by no means as lavish as she had hoped. She refused it not because she didn't need it, but because she was engaged in a public relations operation of her own. It was the training of her daughter, Alexandra, to take such a place in the royal hierarchy that she would never be subjected to the snubs and setbacks which had been Marina's own lot.

As part of the payment for the royal subsidy to her household, Princess Marina had often functioned at openings or occasions which might otherwise have required the presence of the Queen, the Queen Mother or Princess Margaret, and these she had performed uncomplainingly; though the only ones she had really enjoyed were those which involved philharmonic concerts or tennis at Wimbledon. Soon, quite obviously, for what these occasions need is youth and glamour, her daughter would be expected to take her place; and she must be trained to dress for the part, to look as if she were enjoying them, to exude the atmosphere of regality and youth which is a sure way to excite public attention.

But would she ever be more than a second- or third-string player in the royalty game?

Despite all the training which she was given – how to look her best, how to be always caught smiling, how to keep her shoulders well held back, how to lope easily but not too seductively on her long legs – there is not much doubt that she would have remained in the minor leagues of royal activity, along with the Harewoods, her brothers and their wives, had not Princess Margaret got herself emotionally involved to the extent that she expressed a wish to opt out of all her regal activities.

The crisis over Princess Margaret and Group Captain Townsend was, for the planners at the Palace, a practical problem rather more than an emotional crisis. They had to plot the programme of the Royal Family with the idea kept well in mind that Princess Margaret (like Singapore during the last war) was about to be lost. Which bastion of royal privilege could be promoted into taking her place?

The planners went to work on Princess Alexandra and found that her perfervid advocates, Marina and Sir Philip Hay, had already developed her to the extent that, as Alexandra described it later, 'I was operational.' How effectively remained to be seen, and was.

It has been mentioned before that Princess Margaret has never made any secret of the fact that she relishes her royal role, and it is a measure of her devotion to the two loves of her life, Townsend and Snowdon, that she was prepared during the emotional crises concerning them to give up her position rather than her men.

What was a convulsive period of unhappiness and strain for Margaret was regarded as a period of necessary adjustment and preparation by the advisers at the Palace, and as an opportunity for Alexandra by her mother. Princess Marina and Princess Margaret have never been close friends or confidantes, and there was therefore no compunction felt at Iver in pushing Alexandra forward as the logical successor to the Queen's sister as the glamour girl to be exploited by the royal planners.

In the event, Princess Margaret sacrificed Group Captain Townsend to her royal role, more in response to pleas from those she trusted (or thought she did) than her own instincts; and in her unhappiness it was not perhaps unnatural that she turned her scorn on the young princess who had been groomed to take her place. Someone (making a play on the fact that Alexandra lived with her mother at Coppins, Iver) even wrote a skit called 'Barbara Alexandra of Carbon-Coppins'.

It hurt at the time, but it made no difference to the fact – as soon became apparent – that Alexandra was no substitute for Margaret but a personality in her own right, and a welcome one indeed. She had a combination of qualities which the

British love – a boyish and gangling nervousness, plus an anxiety to please, plus a super-abundant concentration of simple sex-appeal.

It was probably Princess Marina's close friend, Cecil Beaton, aided and abetted by her other astute friend, Noël Coward, who told Princess Marina to tell her daughter:

'Don't make an enemy of the photographers. Make each cameraman your friend. Smile at the man who takes the picture, and the image will be imprinted on his lens.'

From the start of her tours abroad Princess Alexandra was encouraged by her mother and by Philip Hay to do her best for the cameramen accompanying her, and never has a policy worked better. During her visit to South America she was never once shown from a wrong angle, as she might have been, principally because Princess Marina regularly approached the cameramen and asked whether they had taken the pictures they wanted, and whether they needed more.

A picture of Princess Alexandra and Robert Haswell during the Princess's tour of Central and South America in 1960. Colleagues rudely captioned it: 'I'll give you a dollar for that camera!'

There was one moment during her Far East tour when one photographer, much to his astonishment, guilty delight and dismay, found himself in such a position that he had a clear and uncompromising view of Princess Alexandra undressing for her evening bath, and could easily have taken pictures of it. It is a measure of his admiration for her that he didn't even succumb to the temptation to do it for his private edification, and that he spent the next half-hour keeping his colleagues away from the same vantage point.

There is no doubt that what appeals to all who watch Princess Alexandra in public is her naturalness, her spontaneity, her eagerness to be thought one-with-you rather than one apart. There is no doubt that much of her success in royal circles comes from the support and sponsorship of Prince Philip, not simply because he comes from the same Greco-Danish background as she does, not because he and Princess Margaret have a slightly abrasive relationship,[1] and that he therefore wants to promote his cousin at the expense of his sister-in-law, but because she really is a star in her own right.

But there are also moments when Philip probably resents her easy, almost automatic success with those elements of publicity with which he has such a difficult relationship. How can Alex get on so well and so easily with those terrible cameramen, who cause him so much trouble?

No better example of it could be given than during her tour of the Far East. At one point Princess Alexandra was taken to a spot in the New Territories in Hong Kong which looks down into Communist China, and after taking pictures of her staring across the frontier the two photographers with her – from rival newspapers – set up their apparatus to take a long view over the terrain. She went over to gaze through the viewfinder of one and, while doing so, inadvertently pressed the trigger.

'Do it again,' said the cameraman (who was representing the London *Daily Mirror*), and she did so.

Meanwhile, Robert Haswell, of the *Daily Express*, was standing by looking

1. There is one story that in the early days of his marriage to Princess Elizabeth, before she became Queen, Prince Philip had a desk made for himself at Clarence House and included in it a hidden compartment opened by a secret device in the woodwork. One day the workman employed to fix it was surprised by Princess Margaret who demanded to know where the secret panel was concealed, and was not a little aggrieved when she was refused. The workman got a bonus from Philip for his adamant attitude.

Lord Snowdon (or Mr Anthony Armstrong-Jones, as he then was) usually took the official birthday pictures of Princess Alexandra, but in 1959 he was in the United States on an assignment for the *Daily Express*. So Alexandra and her mother, Princess Marina, decided to call in a Press photographer, and chose Robert Haswell. These are the pictures he took at Kensington Palace, to the accompaniment of songs from Alexandra's favourite singer, the late Nat King Cole

Two pictures which capture exactly the exuberant quality of spirit which Princess Alexandra projects. Both were taken (though on different occasions) when she visited the Women's Institute near her mother's home at Iver, Bucks

Princess Alexandra had a tremendous success during her tour of Mexico in 1959, not a little of it due to the superintendence of her mother, Princess Marina, who accompanied her. Here she is at an official banquet in Mexico City

In 1960 Princess Alexandra, fresh from h
success in Mexico, was asked to go to We
Africa. This time she went alone, and h
mother, who had nursed her through her fi
official occasions, stayed at home. She was ju
as big a success as ever

Princess Alexandra with her mother,
Princess Marina, and a tiny Mexican
caballero

Princess Alexandra has always been a favourite with the cameramen who accompany royal tours, for she goes out of her way to make sure that they get the shots they want. In addition she is, of course, potently photogenic. These pictures were made by Haswell during her first Far East tour in 1961. *Above:* The Mayor of Hong Kong shows her how to handle chopsticks. *Right:* She shows the mayor how to handle a princess. *Opposite:* They set off for a floating restaurant in Hong Kong

Japan's famous cultured pearls are produced on the Inland Sea near Ise. The pearl-divers who gather in the harvest from oysters planted on the sea-bed are all girls. They are not normally as well-clad as they are shown in these pictures, but were specially draped by the Japanese for Alexandra's visit. *Right:* She feeds the deer in a park near Kyoto

Princess Alexandra visits a Japanese teahouse for a tea ceremony in Kyoto

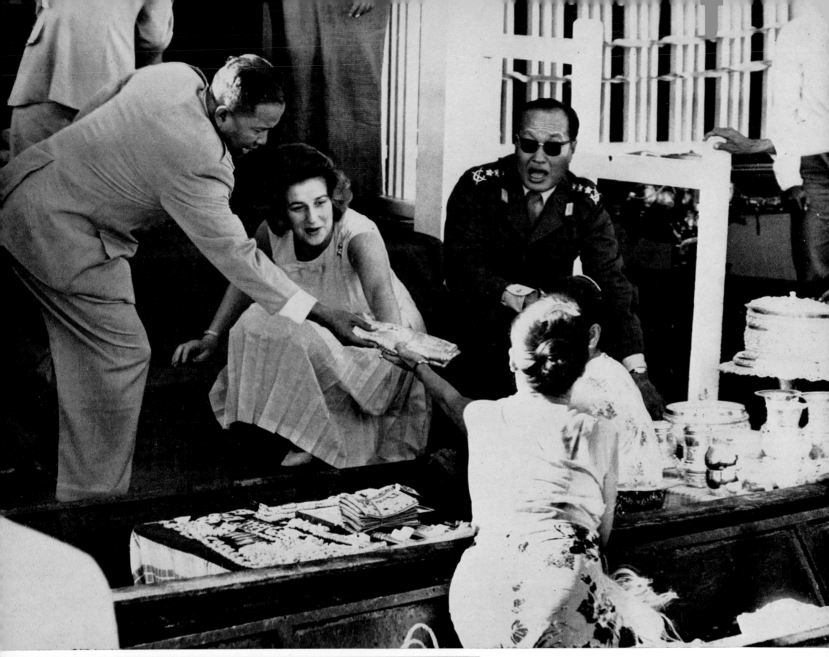

After a water festival in the Shan States of Northern Burma Princess Alexandra accepts an offering from a floating 'gift shop'

A visit to the Shwe Dagôn pagoda in Rangoon – and an official opportunity for a girl to take her shoes off

During the honeymoon of Princess Alexandra and Mr Angus Ogilvy at Marbella, Southern Spain, in 1963, they consented to give an hour of their time on the beach for a photographic session with Haswell. These delightful pictures are the result. They are so natural, in fact, that one British newspaper accused Haswell of having 'snatched' them

128

extremely unhappy. But not for long. Quickly realising the implications of her reflex action, Princess Alexandra came across to Haswell's camera and took some pictures through his viewfinder too. It is an unusually quick-thinking princess who can work it out so that, as happened in this case, rival newspapers were able to come out with pictures the following morning under the headline:

ALEX TAKES OUR PICTURE OF RED CHINA

Haswell is the only Fleet Street photographer who, alone, has taken an official birthday picture of a member of the Royal Family, and it was, of course, of Princess Alexandra who chose him because she trusted his discretion and admired his skill. Normally the official pictures of royalty are taken by a roster of closely vetted studio men, not all of them as expert or as inspired as their publicity might indicate. In this case Lord Snowdon (or Anthony Armstrong-Jones as he then was) had been engaged to take Alexandra's birthday portrait, but he was away in New York on assignment for the *Daily Express* and had excused himself. Robert Haswell asked to do the assignment in his place, and, to his astonishment, was accepted – astonished, I may say, not because he felt he was incapable of the job but because of the Palace attitude towards Fleet Street cameramen.

He carried out his task with considerable success, some of his most human shots being taken to the accompaniment of a disc of Alexandra's favourite singer, Nat King Cole. The pictures went all over the world and had an enormous success. But though on this occasion the experiment of having a news photographer take live pictures was repeated, subsequently Sir Philip Hay and Princess Marina were severely rebuked from the Palace for allowing a *newspaper* – rather than a studio – photographer in the house. What next?

Alas, even someone as bold and experimental as Princess Alexandra is not sufficiently brave to withstand Buckingham Palace disapproval of experiment; and after her marriage to Mr Angus Ogilvy not even she had the courage to demonstrate how easily a situation can be overcome if only the co-operation rather than the competitiveness of the newspapers is sought.

Her honeymoon was spent on the south coast of Spain near Marbella, and just as the Queen and Prince Philip had satisfied all demands upon their time by allowing one picture, and no more, of her relaxing with her husband, so Princess Alexandra hoped to do the same. A few days after the honeymoon began Robert Haswell was approached by Mr Angus Ogilvy and an arrangement was made that the following day pictures would be allowed of the couple enjoying themselves on the beach.

There seems to be no harm in revealing now that Alexandra and her husband made a condition. Would Haswell please arrange the taking of his photographs so that they would appear to have been 'snatched' rather than posed or taken with consent? He did not go into the reasons why, but it was quite obvious that the Palace officials who had objected to 'intrusive' Fleet Street cameramen being invited into a royal home might also object to a permissive attitude towards a honeymoon photograph. What the Queen had allowed was not necessarily a precedent.

So Haswell took his attractive and happy photographs of the royal honeymooners as if they were entirely ignorant of his presence, and then spent the next half-hour taking the two of them through the lens of Alexandra's new miniature Minox camera, a wedding gift. Two days later he was attacked by a national newspaper as a rude and ruthless intruder on royal privacy and couldn't say a word about it. Princess Alexandra and her husband are, however, no longer so vulnerable today.

That is because this tall young woman of such effervescent – but not entirely effortless – charm has won her place among the Royals as a star of the show in her own right. The time has passed when she need be considered any longer as a mere substitute for her not so dearly beloved cousin, Princess Margaret; and the time has passed, too, when Princess Margaret should be suspected of sneering or diminishing her. If ever the claws were out, they have now been sheathed. Both are intensely practical women, experts by now in the business of royalty, and they realise that they complement rather than compete with each other.

So long as they continue to sparkle – and why should they not? – they will be jewels in Britain's crown.

It would be disingenuous to suggest that anyone else matters nowadays in the royal entourage. The Queen Mother has all but retired to salmon-fish with her memories in the quiet reaches she has achieved since the death of her husband. The

Duke of Gloucester and his Duchess have never penetrated the consciousness of the public except as a couple of decent but unnoteworthy people. The Harewoods are bright, intelligent, avid and up-to-date, but somehow not regal. So far as Princess Marina's other offsprings are concerned, someone once said:

> 'The Girl of Kent
>   is rich, strong ale
> But there's less taste
>   to the Kentish male.'

He was a male himself, of course, and therefore possibly prejudiced. None the less, the Royals are really only four strong until their children grow, and it is through this quartet that the image of the Monarchy is projected. It is a matter of rejoicing that it is Queen Elizabeth the Second, and not any of the others, who calls the tune.

Call me ma'am

Earl Attlee once described the occupant of the throne as 'a kind of referee, although the occasions when he or she has to blow the whistle nowadays are very few'.

It is an inelegant description to apply to Queen Elizabeth, and an inapt one, too, for her duties and her preoccupations nowadays are considerably more than keeping an impartial eye on squabbling politicians. Alas, the monarchical set-up does not include the provision whereby the Queen's subjects can award her some sort of decoration, in the same way that she bestows them on her subjects, but the four-teenth year of her reign would seem to be the moment to indicate that she has earned and deserved one.

It seems remarkable in the mid-sixties to remember that only five or six years ago a concentrated propaganda campaign was being waged in Britain against the Monarchy, and British writers of skill and reputation were doing their best to denigrate the system in magazines and on television overseas. True, the object of the attack was the system rather than the individual, but how could you shoot at one without hitting the other? Among young people, and in Left-Wing political circles, the anti-royalist polemics expressed a prevailing mood of cynical disen-chantment with what they considered to be an outmoded institution whose main purpose was to bolster privilege and uphold the Tories. The organiser of one public opinion poll who conducted a private – and admittedly limited – sampling of national opinion of the Royal Family discovered no large proportion of republican sentiments but an enormous wedge of complete indifference or cynical antipathy.

135

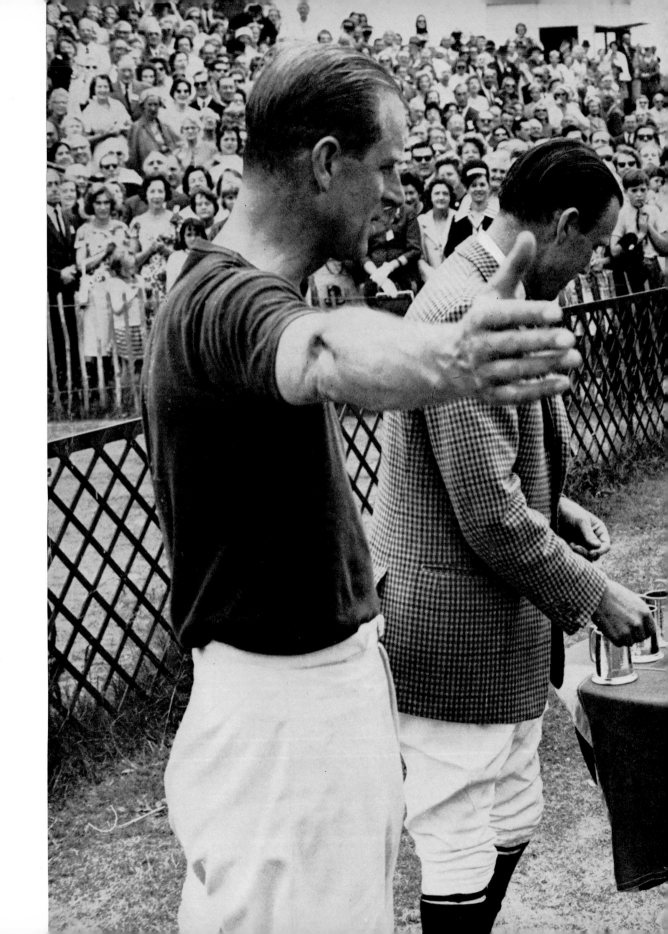

The Queen (Prince Philip to her far right) presents the prizes after a polo tournament at Smith's Lawn, Windsor

137

That the mood has changed is due almost entirely to the efforts of the Queen. A year or two ago the criticisms of 'that extravagant young lady' Princess Margaret, or the murmurs against the outspokenness of Prince Philip, would have been used as a launching pad for some pyrotechnical attacks on the throne itself. But no more. Queen Elizabeth is not only not attacked by the Left and sneered at by the young, she is actually praised by them both. The reason for it is by no means because she is a referee who rarely blows her whistle, but because she blows it a good deal of the time.

The five prime ministers who have served under her have all come to respect the intensity of her interest, and the later ones have begun to realise that her knowledge and experience of certain constitutional items is considerably more mature than their own. This is hardly surprising. There have been four Presidents of the United States and three rulers of Russia while she has occupied the throne, and she has been concerned in crises with all of them.

'She does her homework,' said one Premier, with grudging admiration, after emerging from one audience during which 'she pinned me to the wall with her questions'. Her father, King George the Sixth, used to complain that 'no one ever tells me anything', but his daughter has from the start demanded to know what ideas were in the minds of her ministers, what policies they were pursuing, and what were the possible consequences. It is no secret that she has taken as the model for the attitude she should assume towards public affairs that of her grandfather, King George the Fifth, who always considered it his duty to be a judge there to see justice done to *all* of his people rather than those represented by the party in power.

As Sir Harold Nicolson's biography of him reveals, he intervened twice during the General Strike of 1926 to prevent the Tory Government's extremer elements from introducing punitive measures against the strikers. Though his own political convictions were almost undoubtedly Tory, as were those of his friends and advisers, and though his knowledge of middle- and working-class Britain was remote, he tried hard to think for them and 'protect' them.

It is a measure of Elizabeth's even greater success in her role as influencer and arbiter that, during the Rhodesian crisis of 1965–6, when the Labour Prime Minister, Harold Wilson, at one time saw the Queen six times in one month, not even the most perfervid diehard suggested that she was being affected in her opinions by the Premier – although they were equally sure that that was what the Premier was trying to do. Elizabeth, as some ministers have found to their cost, has a mind of her own and it is a good one. Neither flattery nor cajolery can affect the coolness of her judgment, and 'she knows what's going on'. Whether a Government be of the Left or the Right, she has now convinced them that her attitude will be the same and her intentions unchanged: that though the Premier who comes to see her is young or old, Labour or Tory, her job is to make sure that they are working for the common good, that they are eschewing the excesses of party spirit. True, she cannot constitutionally force them to curb excesses, but she can force them to listen and bear her admonitions in mind.

'When she expresses an opinion,' said a minister, 'she has all the magisterial aplomb of Queen Victoria. Pray God she never gets to be as dictatorial.'

It is not likely that she ever will.

Nor is it likely that she will ever be moved to confide in, and be influenced by, her First Gentleman of the Realm as Victoria was by her Prince Consort. For she is a much shrewder and worldlier woman.

This is what some members of the royal entourage still cannot understand: that the Queen can possibly compartmentalise her life, and keep one vital portion of it private from Prince Philip; that on matters of national interest she neither seeks advice from her husband (but only from her ministers) and would reject it if it were given. That is why anyone sending a note to Prince Philip saying: 'Please show this to Lilibet' ensures that it never reaches her, since Prince Philip would never let her see it – and realises that she would ignore it if he did.

For he, more than anyone, knows that there is a part of his wife's life that he cannot share, powerful though he may nowadays be in the system. He not only has no say when large national crises arise, but he is not even kept *au fait* with what is going on, as the Queen certainly is. And that is by the Queen's own decision. Some years ago, one Prime Minister suggested to the Queen that, since Philip was her husband, and father of her children, and played an increasing public role, he should be allowed to share with her the privilege accorded otherwise to no one except members of the Cabinet: that he be allowed to see State papers.

The Queen said no. She gave no reason for it. But she said no. As a wife, she cannot have found it an easy decision to have made; but as Queen it was obviously the only one possible.

One of the most unfortunate results of the inept public relations organisation at Buckingham Palace is its failure to convey this formidable and phenomenally resolute character which Queen Elizabeth possesses. She does not even allow her intimates to fool or flatter her. She is a power-house of energy but, with the art that conceals art, manages to convey the simple ease of everything she does. She does at least four jobs and does them remarkably well: she is a wife and mother; she is the Head of the State, with all that means in the way of audiences with her ministers, Privy Councils, keeping up with her 'homework'; she is Head of the Commonwealth, a tricky tight-rope walk in these days of inter-racial and inter-Commonwealth conflict; and she is the Queen the public sees on State and charity occasions, with never a hair out of place and seldom a frown on her face.

The pace and the strain are enormous, and few other women would have the stamina to stand up to it. That she does so with such grace and outward equanimity is something which premiers and presidents have come to envy. Her serenity is a virtue which her advisers dearly wish was possessed by her husband and her sister; but she is less distressed than they are when these two put their foot in it, for she understands some of the frustrations they must feel. For they will always be subordinates, and she – thank God – is Head of the Firm.

Jumble sale at Braemar

The time for their subjects to see the Royal Family at their most relaxed is when they holiday in Scotland. These scenes show them enjoying themselves in a completely unself-conscious way, among the people they know, like, understand. They were taken at a jumble sale held at Braemar in aid of the Crathie Church rebuilding fund, and for the tourists who had driven there in a hope of a glimpse of the Queen ('she's bound to look in for a short time, anyway') there was a bonanza reward. Not only was the Queen there but also Prince Philip, Princess Margaret, Prince Charles and Princess Anne.

Unexpectedly, they decided to liven up the proceedings and increase the takings by doing some selling themselves. What followed was a fascinating display of the differences in regal sales technique. No nonsense – and no quarter – from Prince Philip; and no change either, whether you handed over a ten or twenty-shilling note. Sheer radiating sex-appeal from Princess Margaret. A charming eagerness to please from Charles and a shy, daffy, mock-helplessness from Anne.

As for the Queen, she waded into the job with the method and efficiency she gives to everything she undertakes. Business was so brisk that Queen Elizabeth took off the jacket she was wearing and hung it up. It wasn't until an hour later that she discovered one of her helpers was trying to sell it! Chief Inspector Perkins recovered it just in time. The Queen's remark: 'Phew! That was a close one!'

143

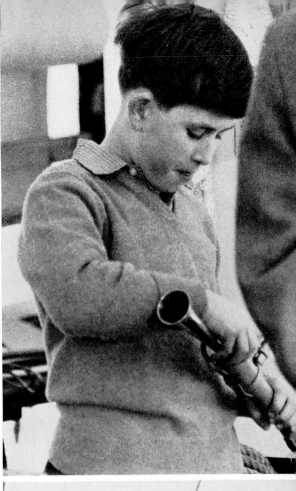

Princess Anne watches the takings roll in; Prince Charles finds an interesting piece of jumble, and Inspector Perkins hangs up the jacket the Queen nearly lost

'Sheer, radiating sex-appeal' from Princess Margaret

The royal fur coat comes under admiring scrutiny at Ascot as the Queen walks in the paddock with the Duke of Norfolk. It is rare to catch the Queen in a sombre mood, especially at the races, but here (*left*) is an exception. Princess Margaret, the Duchess of Gloucester and Princess Alexandra look pensive too. Can the royal favourite have lost?

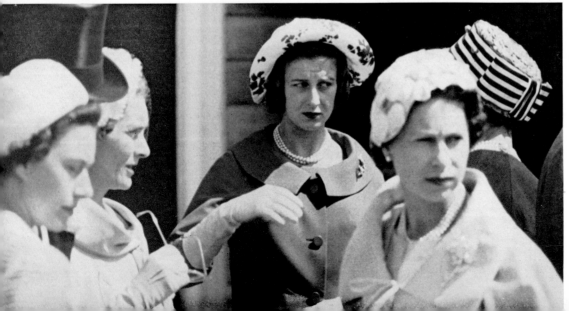

The only time the Queen has led in a horse at Epsom was in 1957, when Lester Piggott, riding Carrozza, won the Oaks. Trainer Murless is patting the horse and Princess Margaret is behind him

The royal guests carry the flag

In 1957 the Queen and Prince Philip made a State visit to France and toured several provincial cities, including Lille, where Haswell took this picture. *Right:* They drive in cavalcade along the Champs Élysées to the Arc de Triomphe and the tomb of France's unknown warrior

On October 21st, 1958, the Queen and Prince Philip visited the German Embassy in London for the first time since the war. They were there to dine with President Heuss of Germany, who was paying a State visit to England

Right: At a Scout occasion at Windsor in 1961 Robert Haswell produced this picture of the Queen, one of his best-liked

On their State visit to Rome in 1961 the Queen and Prince Philip are received at the gates of the Vatican as they arrive to see the Pope, the first time a British monarch had done so. *Left:* On the steps in front of the Vittorio Emmanuele monument on Capitol Hill, Rome, with Italian government officials

The Queen had an umbrella ready to protect herself and her guest as they drove through London during the State visit of President Tubman of Liberia in 1962

Left: The Queen is received by President Gronchi

All smiles at Badminton

Some of the happiest and most unconventional photographs of the Royal Family are those taken at the Badminton Horse Trials. Here are some of them. Except for Prince Philip, who prefers other kinds of horse sports, the Royals seem to respond with enthusiasm to the people, the atmosphere, the jumping itself. Even though the weather is usually bad, it seems not to affect their spirits

Badminton vignettes featuring the Queen, the Queen Mother, Prince Charles, Princess Anne and Lord Snowdon. (Since he joined the Royal Family, their interest in photography has quickened, and the quality of their pictures has vastly improved)

A pensive moment for the Queen while attending the horse trials at Badminton. The rose she holds has just been handed to her by one of the judges

Princess Margaret and Lord Snowdon stroll in the grounds

The Queen drives to Smith's Lawn, Windsor
Great Park, to watch her husband at polo

The Queen at the christening of the child of Mr David and
Lady Pamela Hicks

Right: The Countess of Athlone and Earl Mountbatten
came to admire, too

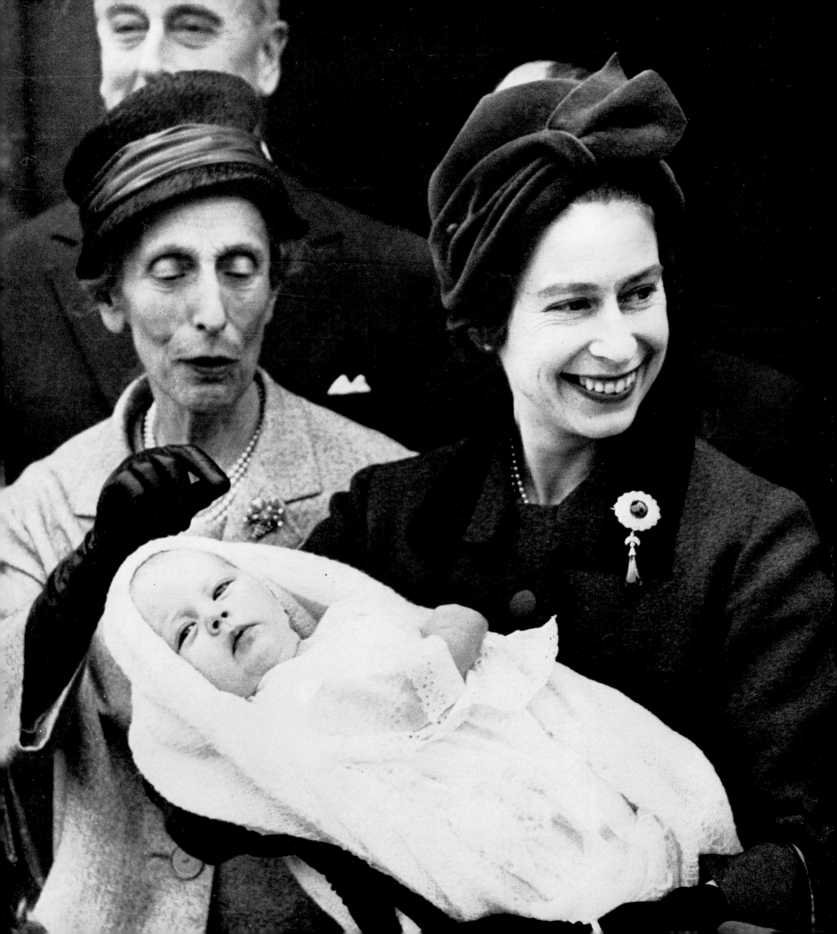

The Queen at the dedication of Coventry Cathedral in 1962

Left: The Queen and Prince Philip at a Garter ceremony at Windsor

A famous picture by Robert Haswell which delightfully demonstrates that even royalty cannot always maintain their 'royal faces', especially when they have been waiting around for a long time. It was taken at the wedding of Princess Alexandra and Mr Angus Ogilvy in 1963. But, as can be seen from the subsequent pictures, the moment of weariness did not last long and, a few minutes later, Haswell secured some really animated pictures of Princess Margaret and Lord Snowdon

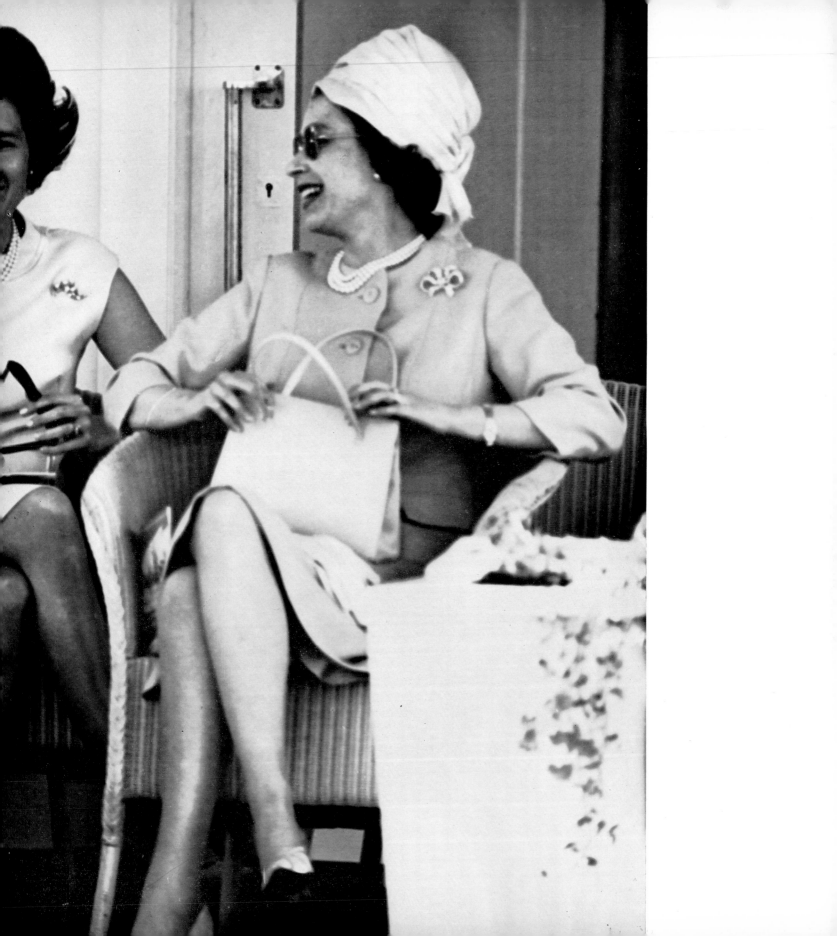

During a polo match at Windsor: the
Queen relaxes with a friend and, *above*,
listens to Earl Mountbatten of Burma

'The Head of the Firm'